# THE QUALITY OF LIFE IN LONDON

# The Quality of Life in London

Edited by

A. H. HALSEY
ROGER JOWELL
BRIDGET TAYLOR

# Dartmouth

Aldershot • Brookfield USA • Singapore • Sydney

Published by
Dartmouth Publishing Company Limited
Gower House
Croft Road
Aldershot
Hants GU11 3HR
England

Dartmouth Publishing Company
Old Post Road
Brookfield
Vermont 05036
USA

**British Library Cataloguing in Publication Data**
Quality of Life in London
  I. Halsey, A.H.  II Jowell, Roger.  III Taylor, Bridget.
  301.09421

**Library of Congress Cataloging-in-Publication Data**
The quality of life in London / edited by A.H. Halsey, Roger Jowell
  and Bridget Taylor.
      p.    cm.
    Includes bibliographical references and index.
    ISBN 1-85521-676-0
    1. Quality of life–England–London. 2. London (England)-
  -Economic conditions. 3. London (England)–Social conditions.
  I. Halsey, A.H.  II. Jowell, Roger.  III Taylor, Bridget.
  HN398.L7Q35   1995
  306'.09421'2–dc20                                             95-1651
                                                                   CIP

ISBN 1 85521 676 0

Printed in Great Britain at the University Press, Cambridge

# Contents

*Preface*                                                                ix

*Notes on contributors*                                                  xi

**CHAPTER 1. THE QUALITY OF LONDON LIFE**
by Howard Davies ...        ...        ...        ...        ...        ...        ...        **1**

    Introduction        ...        ...        ...        ...        ...        ...        1
    Transport        ...        ...        ...        ...        ...        ...        3
    Education        ...        ...        ...        ...        ...        ...        4
    Healthcare        ...        ...        ...        ...        ...        6
    Public space and civility        ...        ...        ...        ...        ...        7
    The 'Vision Thing'        ...        ...        ...        ...        ...        9
    Conclusion        ...        ...        ...        ...        ...        10
    *References*        ...        ...        ...        ...        ...        ...        11

**CHAPTER 2. EMPLOYMENT ISSUES**
by Ian Gordon        ...        ...        ...        ...        ...        ...        ...        **13**

    Introduction        ...        ...        ...        ...        ...        13
    The London economy        ...        ...        ...        ...        ...        14
    Labour market conditions in London        ...        ...        15
    Problems        ...        ...        ...        ...        ...        18
    Diagnoses of the problems        ...        ...        ...        ...        21
    Policy initiatives        ...        ...        ...        ...        ...        25
    Some issues for investigation        ...        ...        ...        ...        29
    Directions for policy        ...        ...        ...        ...        ...        30
    *Notes*        ...        ...        ...        ...        ...        ...        31
    *References*        ...        ...        ...        ...        ...        ...        32

**CHAPTER 3. CRIME IN LONDON:  AN ASSESSMENT**
by Mike Hough and Pat Mayhew     ...     ...     ...     ...     **35**

    Crime in London - the shape of the problem     ...     ...     35
    Comparisons with the rest of England and Wales     ...     ...     36
    International comparisons     ...     ...     ...     ...     36
    Crime trends ...     ...     ...     ...     ...     ...     38
    Public disorder     ...     ...     ...     ...     ...     39
    Public concerns about crime ...     ...     ...     ...     39
    Attitudes to the police     ...     ...     ...     ...     40
    Crime in London:  a summary     ...     ...     ...     ...     41
    Crime-related issues in the London/New York survey     ...     42
      Victimisation     ...     ...     ...     ...     ...     42
      Other crime-related questions     ...     ...     ...     ...     43
    *Notes*     ...     ...     ...     ...     ...     ...     43
    *References*     ...     ...     ...     ...     ...     43
    *Appendix*     ...     ...     ...     ...     ...     ...     45

**CHAPTER 4. PUBLIC SPACE AND CIVILITY IN LONDON**
by Ken Young     ...     ...     ...     ...     ...     **47**

    Introduction: rediscovering the urban public realm     ...
    47
    Public space and the urban public realm     ...     ...     ...     50
    Public and private space in London     ...     ...     ...     52
    Urban change and civility     ...     ...     ...     ...     56
    Encounters in public space     ...     ...     ...     ...     57
      Role differentiation     ...     ...     ...     ...     ...     58
      Impersonality     ...     ...     ...     ...     ...     59
      Bystander distancing     ...     ...     ...     ...     ...     60
    Conclusion: towards a new view of urban renewal     ...
    61
    *Notes*     ...     ...     ...     ...     ...     ...     62
    *References*     ...     ...     ...     ...     ...     63

**CHAPTER 5. TRANSPORT**
by Tony Ridley     ...     ...     ...     ...     ...     ...     **67**

    Introduction     ...     ...     ...     ...     ...     ...     ...     67
    Transport     ...     ...     ...     ...     ...     ...     68
    History     ...     ...     ...     ...     ...     ...     72
    Recent times ...     ...     ...     ...     ...     ...     76
    The London lobby     ...     ...     ...     ...     ...     79
    *References*     ...     ...     ...     ...     ...     80

**CHAPTER 6. HOUSING**
by Christine M E Whitehead     ...     ...     ...     ...     **83**

    Introduction     ...     ...     ...     ...     ...     ...     83
    Definition of the housing problem in London     ...     ...     84
    Some background information     ...     ...     ...     ...     86

How the housing system has operated ... ... ... 90
  Affordability ... ... ... ... ... 90
  Access ... ... ... ... ... 91
  The quality of the stock ... ... ... ... 94
  Investment ... ... ... ... ... 95
Key questions ... ... ... ... ... 97
  The roles of central and local government ... ... ... 97
  Housing associations and other social providers ... ... ... 98
  The private rented sector ... ... ... ... 100
  Land availability ... ... ... ... ... 100
  Access and capacity to pay ... ... ... ... 101
Current policy initiatives ... ... ... ... 102
*Note* ... ... ... ... ... 104
*References* ... ... ... ... ... ... 104

**CHAPTER 7. EDUCATION**
by Donald Naismith ... ... ... ... ... ... **107**

The national background ... ... ... ... 107
  The problem ... ... ... ... ... 107
  Schools matter ... ... ... ... ... 108
  The 'sociological' approach ... ... ... ... 109
  The government's response ... ... ... ... 110
  A 'Consumerist' approach to education ... ... ... ... 111
London's position ... ... ... ... 112
  The background to change ... ... ... ... 112
One borough's response: Wandsworth's ... ... ... 115
  Primary education ... ... ... ... ... 116
  Primary standards ... ... ... ... ... 117
  Secondary education ... ... ... ... ... 118
  Secondary standards ... ... ... ... ... 119
  The ethnic dimension ... ... ... ... ... 120
  Specific grants ... ... ... ... ... 121
  Continuing education ... ... ... ... ... 121
  Special education ... ... ... ... ... 123
  Support services ... ... ... ... ... 123
  The teachers ... ... ... ... ... 124
The government's programme ... ... ... ... 125
Difficulties in the way ... ... ... ... 126
Ways forward ... ... ... ... ... 127
The issues ... ... ... ... ... 128
*References* ... ... ... ... ... 128
*Appendix* ... ... ... ... ... 130

**CHAPTER 8. A VIEW OF LONDON LIFE**
by A H Halsey ... ... ... ... ... ... **135**

Four themes ... ... ... ... ... 140
Another Easter Monday ... ... ... ... ... 146

The Archbishop's Commission ... ... ... ... 151
Concluding remarks ... ... ... ... ... 151
*References* ... ... ... ... ... ... 152

**SUBJECT INDEX** ... ... ... ... ... ... ... **155**

# Preface

The essays that make up this work were produced for a seminar in London in March 1992, funded by the Commonwealth Fund of New York and convened by Social and Community Planning Research (SCPR). The idea behind the seminar was that much could be learned from a comparison of the quality of life in London and New York. A comparable set of papers by British and American authors about London and New York respectively were thus presented at the seminar. The larger purpose of the gathering was to stimulate a social scientific contribution to intelligent city management in Europe and America and perhaps beyond.

The idea of 'quality of life' in a city is not merely fashionable but is also fundamental in any evaluation of how that city feels to live in and how it treats its citizens and visitors alike. It is an amalgam of many factors, some of which arise from infrastructure, such as decent housing, education, transport and a thriving labour market, and others from partly cultural origins, such as a presence of civility and a sense of security. All these factors are touched upon in these essays. The challenge for the authors was to go beyond mere comparisons of economic indicators and current preoccupations with the use of the market to solve problems in the modern city, and to cover social, political and psychological factors too.

Even so, the idea is not, of course, to attempt a comprehensive evaluation of London as a city. That would require looking at a still wider set of considerations, including aesthetic ones, physical ones, even climatic ones, and would necessarily be intensely subjective. Both the architectural and the ecological dimensions of city life may be expected to occupy a high place in the future discussion of urban policy all over the world. This book sticks to a narrower range of topics to which social science can make a distinctive contribution.

It was originally intended to publish the two sets of papers - about London and New York - in one volume. In the event, however, the New York set of papers was published at almost the same time as the seminar by the Manhattan Institute in a special issue of their magazine (*The City Journal*, Vol. 2, No. 2, Spring 1992). Recognising later the contribution that the London papers could make on their own, we decided to publish them in this separate volume. Readers of the two publications can scarcely fail to notice both similarities and contrasts between London and New York. Not only in their different ways are they both crucial points of immigrant entry into their countries, but they inevitably share many of the contemporary problems of big city life, such as unemployment, poor housing, deteriorating public transport, an overstrained educational system and growing crime. Yet their differences are still more striking. London is more securely the metropolis; it is ancient; it still has a conscious tradition of civic administration and therefore of resistance to market solutions. It was perhaps an unconscious irony that the venue of the seminar was the Council Chamber of the Trade Union Congress.

Yet, different or not, there were certainly common anxieties. For instance, the stark statistic that the number of passengers on New York's public transport has halved between 1945 and 1989, while the number of assaults including robberies and murders had meanwhile gone up 15 times brought a recognition among the Londoners as to what could happen here. A common sense of malaise was expressed in a score of ways, despite a recognition that the scale of each problem was often quite different and that it had arisen from different origins. A common theme, alas, was the lack of any obvious and immediate remedial action.

The case, however, for further enquiry to inform more enlightened debate on these issues was uncontested, and it was with this in mind that we decided to publish these essays.

### Acknowledgements

Our sincere thanks are due to the Commonwealth Fund of New York for funding the seminar that gave rise to this volume, to Howard Davies for chairing it and to Rosemary Peddar of SCPR for organising it. We are also indebted to the American and British discussants whose criticisms and observations helped to improve these papers and to the 60 or so other participants in the seminar who performed much the same role. Finally, we are extremely grateful to Lis Box of SCPR for her usual expertise in typing and preparing the camera-ready copy for this book and to other colleagues in SCPR, in particular Bob Erens, for their role in shaping the project.

A.H.H
R.J.
B.T.

# Notes on contributors

**Howard Davies** is Director-General of the Confederation of British Industry. Formerly he was a civil servant for eight years, first in the Foreign Office and then in HM Treasury. In 1982 he joined McKinsey & Co where he worked on a range of industrial, commercial and financial studies in the UK and overseas; in 1985 he was seconded for a year as Special Adviser to the Chancellor of the Exchequer. From 1987 to 1992 he was Controller of the Audit Commission for Local Authorities in England and Wales (from 1990 including the National Health Service). He is also a non-Executive Director of GKN, and a member of the International Advisory Board of NatWest. He has written for a number of publications including the *Times*, the *Economist*, the *Spectator* and the *Literary Review*. He has an honourary DLitt from Leicester Polytechnic of which he is also a Governor.

**Ian Gordon** is Professor of Geography at Reading University and has research interests in urban and regional labour markets, migration, and urban policy. His publications include *The London Employment Problem*, co-authored with Nick Buck and Ken Young (Oxford: Oxford University Press, 1986) and *Divided Cities: London and New York in the Contemporary World*, jointly edited with Susan Fainstein and Michael Harloe (Oxford: Blackwell, 1992). He is currently co-directing a study of metropolitan competition within the Single European Market.

**A H Halsey** was born in Kentish Town in 1923, brought up in Rutland, attended Kettering Grammar School and, after the Second War, the London School of Economics. He taught at the Universities of Liverpool and Birmingham, made many visits to America, advised the Secretary of State for Education, was first chairman of the Centre for Educational Research and Innovation at Organisation for Economic Cooperation and Development

(OECD) in Paris, and has been a fellow of Nuffield College since 1962, where he has also been Professor of Social and Administrative Studies in the University, and is now Professor Emeritus.

**Mike Hough** is Deputy Head of the Home Office Research and Planning Unit. He has carried out research on the police, the probation service and crime prevention, and has been involved with the British Crime Survey since its inception in 1982. Publications include *Crime and Police Effectiveness,* co-edited with Professor R V G Clarke (Aldershot: Gower, 1980), *Public Attitudes to Sentencing,* co-edited with Professor N Walker (Aldershot: Gower, 1988) and a number of Home Office monographs and journal articles on the British Crime Survey.

**Roger Jowell** is the Director and co-founder of Social and Community Planning Research (SCPR), Britain's largest social research institute. He is also Co-director of CREST (an ESRC Research Centre for Research into Elections and Social Trends) and a Visiting Professor at the London School of Economics. He has co-authored and co-edited many books, including *Can Labour Win? The 1992 Election and Beyond* (Aldershot: Dartmouth, 1994), *How Britain Votes* (Oxford: Pergamon, 1985), *Understanding Political Change* (Oxford: Pergamon, 1991) and eleven volumes of *British Social Attitudes* (Aldershot: Dartmouth, 1994).

**Pat Mayhew** is Senior Principal Research Officer at the Home Office Research and Planning Unit, London. She played a significant part in the development of situational crime prevention (*Designing out Crime*, London: HMSO, 1980) and has been involved in the British Crime Survey since its inception in 1982, on which she has published extensively (see for example, *The 1988 British Crime Survey*, London: HMSO, 1989). Her current interests include international comparisons of crime and she was co-author of *Experiences of Crime across the World* (Boston, Mass: Kluwer, 1989).

**Donald Naismith** is Director of Education at Wandsworth Borough Council in London. Formerly he spent six years as a history teacher at a south-east London comprehensive school. After a spell of administration he became Director of Education at the London Borough of Richmond-upon-Thames, and then at Croydon, before joining Wandsworth. He writes and lectures widely on educational matters.

**Tony Ridley** CBE FEng, is Professor of Transport Engineering at the Imperial College of Science, Technology and Medicine. Formerly, from 1969-1975, he was the first Director General of the Tyne & Wear Passenger Transport Executive; from 1975-1980 he was the Managing Director of the Hong Kong Mass Transit Railway Corporation; from 1980 he was Managing Director of London's Underground system for over eight years; and more recently Managing Director of the Eurotunnel Project. He is a Fellow of the Chartered Institute of Transport and a Vice President of the Institution of

Civil Engineers, and in 1988 he was the first recipient of the Highways Award of the Institution of Highways and Transportation.

**Bridget Taylor** is Research Officer at Nuffield College in the Centre for Research into Elections and Social Trends (CREST). She previously worked at Social and Community Planning Research as co-director of the British Social Attitudes team and as a researcher in the British Election Study team, and has been an editor and contributor to the annual *British Social Attitudes* reports. She was also co-editor of *Can Labour Win? The 1992 Election and Beyond* (Aldershot: Dartmouth, 1994).

**Christine Whitehead**, OBE, is a Senior Lecturer in the Department of Economics, London School of Economics and Director of the Property Research Unit, Department of Land Economy, University of Cambridge. She has worked in housing research for many years concentrating on issues of housing finance and economic policy. She was awarded the OBE for services to housing in 1991. She has recently been involved with the London Planning Advisory Committee Project on London: World City, as well as with a number of projects looking at the role of social housing in London. She writes and lectures widely on housing economics and finance.

**Ken Young** is a Professor of Politics in the University of London and Vice-Principal of Queen Mary and Westfield College. From 1987 to 1990 he was Director of the Institute of Local Government Studies at the University of Birmingham. A former member of the Local Government Boundary Commission, Ken Young's main interests are in local politics, metropolitan history and urban affairs, and he is the author of a number of books on the political life of London since the mid-nineteenth century. He is a regular contributor to SCPR's *British Social Attitudes* reports.

# 1 The quality of London life

*Howard Davies*

## Introduction

It is 9.45 on a cold, dank, November evening. You, and 82,999 others, have watched the England soccer team play out a 0-0 draw with Albania at Wembley, the sometime 'headquarters of world football'. Down Empire Way you shuffle, while fans with Union Jacks painted on their faces urinate in the litter-strewn bushes, ignored by Metropolitan Police officers on horseback, who shout incomprehensible but aggressively toned instructions through their megaphones. Through a dark, concrete tunnel, decorated with obscene graffiti, you reach Wembley Park tube station, where the newly-installed ticket barriers are mysteriously out of action. You make it, finally, to the platform, to learn that because of a points failure at Baker Street there are no Metropolitan line trains and you are advised to make other travelling arrangements ...

It is 6 o'clock on a sunlit June evening. Four hours of thin-sweater evening stretch out ahead of you. Strolling across St James's Park to your club, your ear is drawn to the sound of the band of the Coldstream Guards playing a medley from *Iolanthe*. Easing yourself into a Royal Parks deckchair, you notice a former Prime Minister, now at rest in the House of Lords, savouring a *Cornetto* in the shade of an enormous plane tree. A carriage and four trot down the Mall, carrying Gold Stick in Waiting to his weekly audience with the Mistress of the Bedchamber. Your reverie is broken by a 'Man from a Ministry', with whom you endured Latin at prep. school, tempting you to a pint of *Old Peculier* at the *Sherlock Holmes*, where he invites you to a weekend seminar at Ditchley Park with the Gorbachevs ...

*       *       *

Which sketch paints the truer picture of London life in the 1990s? The London of incivility, where an aggressive, alienated 'underclass' meets a matching response from the forces of order, in the shadowy context of a decaying infrastructure? Or the low-tension London of parks and pubs and open-access entertainment, where day to day business is done with a smile and a handshake?

No doubt similarly contrasting scenes could be painted of life in New York, Paris, or Berlin. But the sharpest contrasts there might be between private and public experiences. London's charm has, in this century at least, been found more in what Ken Young describes as the 'urban public realm' (**Chapter 3**). So perceptions of decline in the quality of life in that realm strike more directly at the heart of the city's competitive advantage. Most middle class Londoners, of course, go neither to Wembley nor Ditchley Park seminars. But they seem afflicted by a vague sense of unease at the declining quality of their experience of public life in the city.

Furthermore, a swing of the pendulum towards 'private affluence and public squalor', even if the resultant mix is still far more egalitarian than in any American city, or even most in Europe, is politically charged. This is particularly so when, in the early post-Thatcher years, all parties are seeking to reposition themselves in their attitudes to public provision of services and public investment in the fabric of city life.

Add in the potent question of city government, with at least some politicians of all parties uncomfortably conscious of a gap where the Greater London Council (GLC) used to be, yet none wishing to be accused of reinventing it, and it is clear that the quality of life in London is a highly-charged subject. Even apparently simple facts like traffic speeds or the volume of litter are matters of ideological dispute.

Correctly identifying the 'London Question' as one whose time had come, London Weekend Television launched a series of London Lectures at the end of 1990. The first two lecturers, Sir Ralf Dahrendorf, late Director of the London School of Economics (LSE) now exiled in Oxford, and Michael Heseltine, then Secretary of State for the Environment and responsible for local government, neatly summarised the opposing arguments.

To Dahrendorf, "The city is going through a bad patch ... London is in danger of becoming a place for the super-rich, the underclass, and the transients" (Dahrendorf 1990). Quoting a survey which showed that 60 percent of Londoners believed that the quality of their lives deteriorated in the 1980s, he draws adverse (to London) comparisons with New York. London "has become an object, and one to be kicked about rather than cherished and looked after". The answer is spelt out less clearly than the problem. But an elected mayor is part of it, to give "a focus of innovation and a sense of direction". So is "support from the Exchequer", and "an imaginative programme for improving the public well-being of the city is needed if it is to remain competitive in Europe and in the world".

For Heseltine, "London has problems - all cities have problems. But the only one unique to London is a dire pessimism that is woefully out of place" (Heseltine 1991). The 1980s was a "dynamic time for London" as the decline in the number of jobs in the capital was halted and reversed. Finding comfort in the interesting statistic that 43 of the top 100 United States law firms have offices in London, he quotes two recent surveys showing that London is by far the preferred business location in Europe for US firms. Dismissing the question of the appropriate structure of government as one for which most of London's citizens have "a healthy disregard", he identifies three areas in which progress must be made: transport, housing and the social fabric. But in each case he sees an optimistic future, as the benefits of an enhanced investment programme begin to be seen, and as the centre of gravity moves, driven by the regeneration of the Docklands and the economic logic of the European Community: "If Europe is now our destiny, the manifestation of that destiny must in large measure arise where the Thames flows east to welcome it".

Some of the gap  between these two positions may be attributed to pure party politics. Of course Michael Heseltine, in the months before an election, had to accentuate the positive. And Dahrendorf, firmly committed to the notion that Thatcherism was creating an irrecoverable underclass, has his own political antecedents to nurture. But a fault line remains. Between those who believe that, taken all in all, and bearing in mind the alternatives London is, well dash it all, not such a bad old town - and those who chronicle with grim satisfaction its decline into incivility, ignorance, ill-health and immobility.

Having erected such a fence, I surely have the right to sit on it. But the posture is not comfortable in the long run. And I believe it is worth attempting to construct a synthesis of these opposing views, based on the insights in the sectoral analyses which follow.

Five problem areas seem generally to be acknowledged: first, the lack of a co-ordinated approach to transportation; second, a growing mismatch between the skills demanded by London's employers and those on offer from its indigenous workforce; third, a distribution of healthcare resources more suited to the interests of the providers than to the needs of the users; fourth, a decline in traditional civil behaviour patterns in public spaces, perhaps prompted by changes in the configuration of those spaces; fifth, the lack of any central structure to address London-wide issues, or which can act as a focal point around which 'big ideas' can gain reality - what might be described in shorthand as the Olympics factor.

What kinds of solution can be imagined for these problems?

## Transport

The frustrated commuter ranks high among *Private Eye*'s "Great Bores of Today". Yet even fictional complaints about British Rail find it hard to catch up with the reality. In one three-month period in the winter of 1991-92, commuters were told that their misery could be attributable to leaves on the line which new rolling stock could not handle, to delays in the delivery of locomotives, to staff shortages (in the depths of a recession) and to "the wrong kind of snow". British Rail's public relations department threatens to put satirists out of business.

London Transport, the managing agency of the underground and the bus network, fares little better. And indeed its own Chairman, at a seminar in June 1991, said that the tube system was "an appalling shambles in danger of collapsing after decades of neglect" (*Sunday Times* 1991). The decay of the underground is more of a cross-class issue in London than it is in New York. The lager lout uses it to get to Wembley - but senior civil servants and city gents are shoulder to shoulder with them on their way across town to Kensington.

A survey carried out for Coopers and Lybrand's report on London's status as a 'world city' (commissioned by the London Planning Advisory Committee and others) showed that intra-city mobility was the infrastructure characteristic on which businesses based in London rated their city significantly lower than did businesses based in other 'world cities' - New York, Frankfurt, Berlin, Tokyo and Paris (Coopers and Lybrand Deloitte 1991). They identified improved transport co-ordination as the most important potential benefit of a new strategic approach to London city governance.

Ridley argues that a new strategic approach may now be about to emerge (**Chapter 5**). Certainly there are signs that the government has accepted the need for reinvestment. In 1991, capital investment in the underground, which fell in the first half of the 1980s, was running at levels more than twice as high as in 1979 in real terms (Institute of Metropolitan Studies 1991). BR investment programmes have similarly been augmented. Public transport, and particularly rail lobbyists, argue that these investment levels are still significantly lower than in other western European economies. Perhaps they are. But they are higher than appreciated by the travelling public.

Ridley argues that a co-ordinated approach is needed. The London Planning Advisory Committee does not seem to carry the weight needed to perform that role. Here the case for new London-wide planning machinery seems strongest. London's problems are different in quantity and quality from those of the rest of the United Kingdom. A different political and management solution is therefore required.


**Education**

This is less obviously so in the case of education. Gordon points out that the London labour market cannot be viewed in isolation, and describes the extent of labour mobility in and out of the capital (**Chapter 2**). He also cautions against a simplistic view of the 'skills gap', showing that "the co-existence of high levels of both vacancies and unemployment in London cannot be explained primarily in terms of a mismatch between the skills and experience of unemployed people and the type of vacancies available". Though London scores worse on education and training in the 'world city' survey (Coopers and Lybrand Deloitte 1991) than the average for other cities, the difference is slight.

Naismith describes the course of recent reforms in the national education system which, after some delays and adaptation, are now essentially in place in London also (**Chapter 7**). These reforms, whatever else they do, significantly reduce the ability of local government to influence the education system, and place the responsibility for improving standards on the schools and colleges themselves, with little external moderation.

While these reforms work through, it would be perverse to argue for a new structural change. And indeed, it may be that the new educational market-place created by the 1988 Education Reform Act stands a better chance of working in London than anywhere else. It is remarkably true, for example, that the Borough of Richmond scored highest among over 100 education authorities in England and Wales on the first national tests of achievement for seven year-olds. Yet about a quarter of the children resident in Richmond nonetheless go on to private secondary schools - one of the highest proportions in the country.

The crisis of London's education system, if crisis there be, is essentially the same crisis as in the rest of the British system, a crisis of low expectations and low achievements, of inefficiency and ineffectiveness in the face of changing market-place demands. The symptoms seem more acute first, because there are large concentrations of professional and managerial families who have fled the state system, and as yet show no signs of wishing to return to it. And second, because concentrations of immigrants and other socially deprived groups can be found in close proximity to high-priced commercial and residential property.

As Naismith describes, the 'solution' offered by the Conservative government involves tighter central control over the curriculum on the one hand, and greater delegation of control and responsibility to the individual school on the other - what in the United States (where it originated) is known as site management - all within the framework of greater choice for individual parents.

This policy prescription is attractive, and offers the prospect of strengthened links between local communities and their schools. It also threatens to weed out chronically poor institutions, which local authorities have been notoriously reluctant to close. My suspicion is however, that this market-place will, in London, need more assistance than elsewhere to establish itself, that effective school governors will be harder to find and will need more help to make themselves effective, and that business school links, such as the US-style compacts described by Gordon, will take longer to put in place and will, in London's dynamic job market, need constant renewal.

A market-failure 'correction kit' along these lines does not seem an unrealistic objective.

**Healthcare**

London's healthcare problem is different in character from that of the rest of the country however, and certainly justifies separate consideration.

It has two elements: first, the problem - which Londoners generally see as an advantage - of over-provision in acute hospitals, most of which are also important teaching centres. In the centre of London, from Hammersmith in the west to Mile End in the east, there are 11 major teaching hospitals. The inner, relatively deprived, areas of London spend 27 percent more per head than similar areas in other English cities. There are considerably more consultants and junior doctors, 17 and 43 per 10,000 consultant episodes respectively, than in England as a whole, where the figures are 12 and 27 respectively (Boyle and Smaje 1992).

Co-existing with this cornucopia of clinicians is a primary healthcare system which is significantly less satisfactory than is found in most other parts of the UK. Robert Maxwell, the Secretary of the King Edward's Hospital Fund for London, has described the problem with great clarity:

> *London has an inheritance of health services that bears all the marks of a fairy godmother with a perverse sense of humour. It has more than its share of teaching hospitals ... offering high standards of acute care in difficult circumstances. On the other hand, London lacks adequate provision for people with chronic mental or physical illness or handicap ... London's primary care is also patchy: good in some places, bad in others and in general at its worst for the most vulnerable groups, like the homeless ... the basic conundrum is that London's health services, for all their real strengths, are not a good match for the health needs of Londoners.* (Maxwell 1990)

There are, for example, more than twice as many single-handed general practitioners, and GPs with lists of under 1,000 patients, than the national average. This is associated with poor premises and low levels of nursing and ancillary services. There are only just over half as many practice nurses and ancillary staff per partnership as the national average. While for London as a whole the health status of the population, as measured by avoidable and premature deaths at least, is not very different from the average for England as a whole, there are real problems and observable differences in the inner city areas, where standard mortality ratios for avoidable deaths are 17 percent higher than average (Benzeval *et al* 1991).

Cynics argue that the continuation of this state of affairs is attributable to two factors. First, the medical profession finds it highly convenient to work in central London hospitals, close to their private patient workbase in Harley Street. And, second, there is no forum in which the healthcare needs of the capital as a whole can be addressed. Four separate Regional Health Authorities cover the Greater London area, meeting in the middle but with extensive hinterlands in the home counties in each case. All have an interest in maintaining their clinical endowment, none is in a position to take a strategic view. To quote Maxwell again, "There is no shared, positive vision of what London's health services ought to be like" (Maxwell 1990). Our mandarin in his deckchair has ready access to specialists - some no doubt members of his club - with international reputations; the football fan more normally finds himself in a run-down GP's waiting room, waiting hours for his sick note.

The reform package introduced in 1990 has thrown the over-capacity problem into sharp focus. Health authorities around London, the traditional source of a large percentage of referrals to central London hospitals, will in future have a financial incentive to use their local hospitals. It is widely expected that this will lead to the closure of at least one large teaching hospital.

But will the funds released by a rationalisation of acute care be reinvested in the primary sector in London, which is the logic of the reform package? Maybe, but maybe not. The structure of health and local authorities in the capital makes effective purchasing of community services extremely difficult. Only 2 of the 13 inner London local authorities share a common boundary with a single District Health Authority and none with a Family Health Service Authority, the purchasers of primary care (Audit Commission 1992a). In these circumstances, it is almost impossible to produce a coherent statement of the health and welfare needs of the population, let alone develop a strategy to meet them. Yet the structure of local government in the capital is excluded from the terms of reference of the Local Government Commission, set up to review structures elsewhere.

Two reviews are in progress, which may generate some answers. The King's Fund Commission on London's acute services will develop a broad vision of the pattern of acute health services that would make sense for London in the coming decade, concentrating on the service requirements of the capital's population (Boyle and Smaje 1992). The government has also asked Sir Bernard Tomlinson to look at the teaching hospital problem (Tomlinson 1992). It seems likely that some kind of structural change will be needed before a more needs-based allocation of resources can be achieved.

## Public space and civility

Londoners do not spend all their time at school, in a doctor's waiting room, or on a crowded tube train - though to some it may seem that they do. And, as Young cogently argues, it is the quality of experience in the spaces between home and work that decisively influences perceptions of the attractiveness of the city as a place to live and work (**Chapter 3**). "Urban public space" he concludes, "also has a major contribution to make to economic revitalisation".

Yet defining the influences on the quality of that space, and the way people perceive them, is tantalisingly difficult.

Crime, or the fear of crime, is certainly a factor. Hough and Mayhew show that in London "fear of crime is higher than in the country as a whole, but roughly comparable to other British cities", and that public attitudes to the police are, "if anything, more favourable than [those] of other big-city residents" (**Chapter 4**). This may be scant consolation to the victim of a rape attack in a South London park at dusk, or to the football supporter abused by a mounted inspector; it does not, however, suggest that there is an uncontrollable crime wave, or a crisis of confidence in the police as is sometimes argued.

But there are other, less tangible, aspects to consider: what Young calls "quality of interactions between people in public spaces". Statistical support for any firm observation in this area is scarce, and Young points to the need for further research. It is widely assumed however, that such change as there has been, has been for the worse. The Coopers and Lybrand study for the London Planning Advisory Committee and others quotes survey evidence to the effect that 50 percent of Londoners have considered moving out of the capital because of what they see to be a deterioration in the quality of life there (Coopers and Lybrand Deloitte 1991). Attempting to interpret the reasons for this vote of no confidence, they say "the available evidence tends to suggest that the reduction of urban stress, over which individuals have little control, must lie at the heart of any strategy to improve the quality of life in the city" (Coopers and Lybrand Deloitte 1991).

They see, as an important element in such a strategy, greater emphasis on the state of London's green spaces. But the built environment must also make a decisive impact. Whitehead maintains that "The vast majority of Londoners are accommodated in reasonable quality housing at prices they can afford" (**Chapter 6**). And businesses in London rate housing availability in the city (no doubt thinking of their executives) highly on an international scale (Coopers and Lybrand Deloitte 1991). But few would contest that there are pockets of acute decay, and large tracts of inner London where the spaces between these reasonable quality dwellings are hostile, or at best uninviting; little which matches the worst urban jungles of New York or the geometric moonscape of Moscow perhaps, but zones in which to wish someone a nice day seems a satirical commentary on the life chances available.

Young optimistically suggests that "there is now recognition among opinion leaders in the relevant professions that the time has come for planning and urban design to respond to the wider questions of civility and citizenship". But we are a long way from devising a planning system which allows that recognition to take tangible shape. An Audit Commission report on development control shows how nebulous the concept of 'quality' is in urban planning, and how difficult it is for a local authority to devise, introduce and enforce a local plan which responds to the wishes of its citizens (Audit Commission 1992b).

Looking forward, the picture is clouded. I suspect that in the future we will be seen to have reached a watershed in the provision of social housing. The era of political landlords, and the numbers game of political parties outbidding each other in their claims about the number of dwellings they aimed to supply, has been left behind. We might be said therefore, to have obeyed the first law of being in a hole: we have stopped digging. But, although many micro initiatives look promising, there is a large and growing gap between the scale of good quality social housing we can afford to produce and the demand for it. The explosion in homelessness in the last few years is just one, albeit the most noticeable, symptom of that gap in provision. The number of homeless households (on the statutory definition) in London had almost doubled since 1987 to over 36,000 by 1991.

The critical housing need therefore, is to harness the successful elements of small scale housing association (and, in some cases, local authority) provision on a much larger canvas, involving tenants in the management and maintenance of their own estates.

On the planning front, the Coopers and Lybrand report calls for an environmental audit of the capital, something which could fit well with Young's suggestion of further work on identifying the characteristics of urban public space which contribute to a perception of quality in city life.

## The 'Vision Thing'

Nothing is easier than to point to the vacuum at the centre of decision-making in London, and to contrast it with the high profile status of Koch in New York, Chirac in Paris, or Popov in Moscow: international figures who personify their cities on the world stage. Figures as politically diverse as Tony Banks, a vocal ex-GLC Labour MP, and Dame Shirley Porter, the Thatcherite former leader of Westminster City Council, have argued the case for a high profile decision-maker for the capital, whether a mayor or, in Dame Shirley's case, a government minister.

But the legacy of the GLC continues to cast a pall over the debate. Having slain the dragon, the Conservatives find it hard to acknowledge that some kind of replacement is needed. So the Conservative London Boroughs' Association's latest contribution is a lengthy analysis of the financial implications of abolition, designed to prove that funds have been saved (London Boroughs' Association 1991). And Labour, aware that a return to the gesture politics and 'rainbow coalition' days of Ken Livingstone reawakens memories they would prefer to consign to oblivion, prefaces its own plans for a new governing structure in London with a disavowal of any intention to return to the GLC (the Labour Party 1990). They talk instead of "a new kind of democratically-elected, strategic authority for London". The Liberal Democrats seem the only party not traumatised by the GLC experience, calling unconditionally for a strategic authority with the "power to co-ordinate and plan on a London-wide basis" (London Region Liberal Democrats 1991).

Somehow, new kinds of strategic authority do not set the pulse a-racing. They conjure up images of working party reports leading to consultative documents debated in off-site strategy workshops which in turn generate discussion papers on which responses from interested parties are requested, preparatory to the drafting of an outline planning framework with advisory status only.

But the strength of the case for some kind of central body is growing. The shambles of London's attempt to prepare a bid for the 2000 Olympics highlighted the capital's inability to pull together at an important time. Two competing consortia failed to agree on the outlines of a case to put to the British Olympic Committee until the twelfth hour, losing out to Manchester almost by default. And this, it should be remembered, was merely the contest to be selected as Britain's bidder, still many stages from being chosen as the Olympic site.

My suspicion is that within a decade there will be a new authority of some kind, whichever party or parties are in power. While the argument that the GLC was an expensive irrelevance may have been won, the argument that no central body of any kind is needed is in the course of being lost. Michael Heseltine, in his lecture on London, was careful not to rule out change, saying only that "No-one wants change for change's sake", and that "the first question that government would have to address would be the extent to which a shuffling of public sector responsibilities from one organisation to another would actually improve the quality of public service" (Heseltine 1991).

Already a number of models have been proposed. The Confederation of British Industry calls for a London Development Agency (Confederation of British Industry London Region 1991). Hillier Parker, a large firm of surveyors, have drawn up a plan for a Central London Planning Agency, led by a Commissioner, who "would at last provide a voice for London" (Hillier Parker 1991). The Agency "would be responsible for formulating a statutory plan for the Central Business District, which would incorporate the characteristics of both a business plan and a traditional land-use plan".

A project on the government of London supported by the Rowntree Fund has sketched seven options for change, ranging from a minister for London in central government, through enhanced arrangements for co-operation between existing authorities to a new directly elected body with a strong mayor (Travers *et al* 1991).

Some of the elements of the debate around these options concern cost (always an important criterion, since there is nothing more calculated to reduce one's quality of life than a large tax bill to support ineffective administration) and administrative tidiness. They need not be rehearsed here. But the papers which follow show that there is also an important 'quality of life' dimension, which should be given a heavy weight in the equation, as Michael Heseltine himself acknowledged. The most difficult task will be to ensure that quality of life for all classes - the Wembley supporter or the Westminster park visitor - is weighed in the balance.

## Conclusion

It is in the nature of enquiries of this kind that their emphasis is on disentangling the different component parts of whatever it is we mean by the quality of life. Yet we experience life in the round. We may be able to provide answers which are helpful to pollsters on the different elements of the mix, but there will almost certainly remain an 'X' factor for all of us, which makes the difference.

Perhaps it is not too fanciful to argue that the same is true of cities themselves. And that 'X' factor might best be described as confidence. The Coopers and Lybrand 'world city' study summarises its section on quality of life as follows:

> *The key quality of life attributes are related to the alleviation and management of stress from living and working in a busy world city. London compares favourably with other world cities on cultural provision and certain aspects of the environment. Yet London appears to be making less concerted effort than other cities to assess its quality of life attributes and to identify where action is needed.* (Coopers and Lybrand Deloitte 1991)

Perhaps, then, like most of us, London just needs a bit of attention from time to time to restore its sense of direction.

# References

Audit Commission (1992a) *Community Care: Managing the Cascade of Change*, London: HMSO.

Audit Commission (1992b) *Building in Quality: a Study of Development Control*, London: HMSO.

Benzeval M, Judge K and New B (1991) Health and Health Care in London, *Public Money and Management*, Oxford: Blackwell (Spring 1991).

Boyle S and Smaje C (1992) Acute Health Services in London - an analysis, King's Fund London Initiative, Working Paper 2 (February 1992).

Confederation of British Industry London Region (1991) A London Development Agency: Optimising the Capital's Assets, Discussion Paper, London: Confederation of British Industry (July 1991).

Coopers and Lybrand Deloitte (1991) *London, World City Moving into the 21st Century*, report for London Planning Advisory Committee and others, London: HMSO (November 1991).

Dahrendorf, Sir R (1990) Does London Need to be Governed? *London Weekend Television Lecture* (6 December 1990).

Heseltine, Rt Hon M (1991) The Future of London, *London Weekend Television Lecture* (12 December 1991).

Hillier Parker (1991) *CLASP Central London Agency for Strategic Planning*, Hillier Parker (April 1991).

Institute of Metropolitan Studies (1991) *London In Prospect*, London: Institute of Metropolitan Studies (May 1991).

The Labour Party (1990) *London Pride*, London: The Labour Party.

London Boroughs' Association (1991) *Financial Consequences of GLC Abolition*, London: London Boroughs' Association (September 1991).

London Region Liberal Democrats (1991) *Changing London for Good*, London: London Region Liberal Democrats (September 1991).

Maxwell R (1990) London's Health Services, *Christian Action Journal* (Autumn 1990).

The Sunday Times (1991) London's burning for decisive action - now (21 July 1991).

Tomlinson Sir B (1992) *Report of the Inquiry into London's Health Service, Medical Education and Research*, London: HMSO (October 1992).

Travers T, Jones G, Hebbert M and Burnham J (1991) *The Government of London*, York: Joseph Rowntree Foundation.

# 2 Employment issues

*Ian Gordon*

## Introduction

Employment availability, work conditions, job security, and the terms of access to jobs are crucial factors in the quality of life of the great majority of the London population, for whom paid employment represents the normal source of income, status, purposeful activity, and social integration. A clear indicator that all is not satisfactory in this regard is the current rate of unemployment in London - 9.6 percent (as at August 1991), rising to about 12.5 percent in inner London.[1] As we shall show, there are other problems also, of which dependence on unstable employment may be the most significant, threatening a re-casualisation of substantial parts of the London labour market.

And yet London is now, as it has been since the 1920s, at the heart of the strongest regional labour market in the UK, where recruitment problems are commonly reported, with a level of GDP per head 27 percent above the national average and with an unrivalled concentration of highly paid professional and managerial jobs.

This paradox is partly a question of *boundaries* in relation to the spatial structure of labour markets in the London region. Even Greater London as a whole is far from being a closed labour market. One in six of its workforce commutes in from the Outer Metropolitan Area and beyond, a significant proportion from 50 or more miles away from central London. Residential segregation, and the related phenomenon of socially selective out-migration, mean that inner London in particular houses a quite disproportionate share of the most vulnerable, least skilled, and poorest members of the London workforce, while a third or more of its administrative and professional workers commute in from the surrounding shire counties. There is room for argument as to whether this spatial arrangement of different segments of the London labour force actually represents a problem, but it does very largely explain why statistics relating to inner area residents display a concentration of employment problems which would not be expected in a city where job levels had actually been increasing in the mid-late 1980s.

## The London economy

The London economy retains several characteristics from a mercantile past, with a predominance of small businesses (mostly in services but historically in craft manufacturing as well) and with face-to-face contact playing an important role in its transactions. Historically its economic base lay in: its position as the seat of government, making it a centre for elite consumption; the dominant international trading position of the port of London; and the related development of the City of London as the first 'global financial centre' (Buck *et al* 1986; Buck and Fainstein 1992; King 1990). In the first industrial age it lacked the immediate access to ores, fuel and other energy sources which supported the successful factory economies of the great northern cities. However, from around the start of this century, as market orientation assumed greater importance for a new generation of industries, London belatedly became a factory economy. It possessed substantial manufacturing employment from the 1920s onwards, a leading role in the 'high technology' industries of that period, and a major share in the factory openings of the 1930s, notably in the Park Royal industrial estate and other sites in industrial Middlesex (now identified as outer west London). For the past 30 years, however, the level of manufacturing employment has been in steady decline, with the loss of one million jobs (falling from a peak of 1.5 million in 1961). One factor in that decline has been the loss of an important import-processing role, following the contraction and closure of port activities within the city (between about 1967 and 1977), which also involved major direct losses of manual jobs in the docks. Another factor in manufacturing decline was the diminishing importance of a central market location for most manufacturing activities as communications improved and population decentralised. Selective dispersal of population also diminished the pool of skilled artisans within the city which had previously been a significant part of its locational advantage (Buck *et al* 1986). However, most of the decline in industrial employment reflects the combination of two other factors. On the one hand, technological changes everywhere lowered the density of employment on the land occupied by industry, so that the output growth required to sustain employment levels involved continuing growth in the areas occupied by industry (Fothergill and Gudgin 1982). On the other hand, within London such additions to industrial land have not been economically feasible, particularly given the competing demands from other sectors with a stronger need for agglomeration. Industrial cost levels in London in terms of transport, rent and wages now appear well above those in most alternative locations (Tyler 1984), but these high costs have to be seen as largely a reflection of the *success* of other sectors of the London economy.

Much of that success rests on the remarkable growth of employment in financial and business services over the same 30-year period. This has been a national (and international) phenomenon which has impacted particularly strongly on London because of its considerable existing employment base, amounting to 0.5 million jobs in 1961. Employment in the sector has grown by some 0.3 million jobs over the subsequent 30 years, but in contrast to the position in manufacturing (where London's de-industrialisation has proceeded much faster than anywhere else) the actual rates of growth of business service employment have not been consistently above the national average. In relation to a shrinking overall level of employment in the city, with a net loss of some 0.6 million jobs over this period the rising share of business service employment - overtaking that of manufacturing in the early 1980s - has been remarkable however.

Over the past decade or so, the sectoral restructuring of the London economy has been further promoted by the enhancement of its role as one of three 'world cities' (with New York and Tokyo) with a concentration of international finance and corporate control functions within an increasingly integrated global economy (Cohen 1981; Friedmann and Wolff 1982; Fainstein *et al* 1992). This role highlights again the significance of agglomeration economies, particularly in relation to flows of information and face-to-face contacts across a range of specialist services for businesses operating in sensitive market environments. The control requirements of major multi-nationals are a key element, but the business economy itself is still largely one comprised of small firms. The same is true of the elite consumer services and fashion producers whose growth has been stimulated by the increasing purchasing power of affluent professionals. The more general pendulum swing toward market-based rather than bureaucratic forms of economic control, which seems to have followed from the less certain economic environment since the late 1970s, is also a trend working to London's advantage. The impact of these developments was, however, exaggerated by the immediate reaction to the 'Big Bang' of financial services de-regulation in 1985 and the late 1980s credit boom. Over-optimism, excess capacity and an office-building boom have since been reversed as the South-East region led the way into national recession from 1989 on. At the start of the 1990s, however, the London economy is clearly in a quite different shape from that evident even ten years earlier, with an employment base much more dependent on the producer service sector, and with much less reason to expect further substantial declines in overall employment.

**Labour market conditions in London**

A review of the key labour market indicators for London as a whole indicates, first, that average money wages are high by UK standards although, when higher housing and transport costs are allowed for, it is not clear that real wages are above those in most other areas. Average gross weekly earnings for full-time London workers in 1990 were almost 30 percent above the national average, and higher than in any other region. The usual differentials can be found, with females and manual workers each having significantly lower earnings. Compared with equivalent groups elsewhere in the UK, however, female workers have tended to do relatively well in London. The same is also true of those in non-manual jobs, largely on the strength of a substantial representation of administrative and professional workers, growing markedly in numbers and pay during the financial services boom of the mid-1980s. However, among those, especially in public services, with fixed national wages augmented by only a modest London allowance, real incomes in the city are likely to be lower than elsewhere, posing some serious problems of recruitment, which have implications for the quality of life of other Londoners via a poorer standard of service delivery. This problem worsened in the late 1980s (before the recession) when housing costs in London moved further ahead of those elsewhere in the country.

Rates of participation in the formal economy are high, with 79 percent of those in the working age groups being economically active in 1989. Until quite recently London participation rates were well above the national average (indeed about the highest in the country), both because of a high proportion of unmarried females, and because married women had relatively high rates of paid economic activity. The rest of the country has caught up, however, (as have the participation rates of all married women) and London participation rates are now very close to the national average. The ratio of full-time to part-time jobs for women is still distinctively high in the city (with 68 percent of women working full time, against 43 percent nationally), however, and London has scarcely experienced the great growth of part-time jobs evident elsewhere through the 1980s. The high rates of participation leave little scope for the existence of a substantial informal and/or criminal economy, such as is evident in New York City. Overall the 1989 Labour Force Survey (LFS) records two percent of working age residents in London as economically inactive 'for no reason', rising to six percent among single people in inner London.

On a residence basis[2] unemployment in London as a whole is presently about one percent above the national average (standing at 8.4 percent in August 1991), and well above the average for the rest of southern England. For most of the past 20 years or so the London rate has been a little below the UK figure. Inner London unemployment has, however, consistently been well above the national average, and is currently about half as high again. Over time, trends in London unemployment have tended to follow the national pattern of change rather closely, having risen sharply from 1979 to 1982, fallen rather more slowly from 1986 to 1989, and again rising sharply from early in 1989 to a current level approaching the 1986 peak. In the current recession London was some months ahead of the national trend, but the rise in unemployment has actually been less sharp than in the outer areas of the South-East region, which have felt the strongest effects of a reversal of the late 1980s credit boom. There has been a steady upward drift, however, in London's unemployment rate relative to other areas since about 1981.

Marked inequalities are evident in the incidence of unemployment by age, race and social class. The 1989 LFS (prior to the current recession) recorded an overall unemployment rate of 6.2 percent among London residents but 8.8 percent for single males, 8.9 percent for ethnic minorities and 12.5 percent among people lacking any formal qualifications. Some of these differentials had clearly narrowed since the upsurge in unemployment at the start of the decade, when the 1981 LFS had indicated that both black/Asian ethnic origins and lack of formal qualifications doubled individuals' chances of being unemployed (Buck and Gordon 1987). Ethnic minorities (particularly Afro-Caribbeans and Pakistanis/Bangladeshis) were still at greater risk of unemployment, and their position may have worsened again in the current recession. But, given that they comprise only 15 percent of the London labour force, it is clear that unemployment is far from being essentially a problem of ethnic minorities. The unqualified, on the other hand, do represent nearly half the unemployed in London.

Areal differences in unemployment within London are very largely a reflection of the residential distribution of individuals with characteristics increasing their chances of unemployment - including, as well as those already mentioned, youth, disability, old age, working in an unstable or declining industry, manual status and being a public sector tenant (Buck and Gordon 1987; Gordon 1989). These differentials have widened significantly during the 1980s, as have those between Greater London and its commuting hinterland where unemployment is substantially lower.

Unemployment is only one aspect of the effects of employment conditions on quality of life. But it was the most important factor in the worsening of the relative position of those in the lower half of the income distribution observed between 1979 and 1985 (Buck 1991). In the bottom three deciles households were more or less permanently dependent on state benefit but in the fourth and fifth deciles rising unemployment had a major impact on living standards during this period.

Quality of employment is also an issue, however. The Greater London Living Standards Survey, undertaken in 1985-1986, provides a unique set of data on workers' perceptions of these conditions, although without the possibility of comparison with other areas.[3] Physical problems including experience of noise, dust or pollution, moisture or damp, vibration, heavy lifting, heat, cold, and bad lighting were variously reported by between 17 percent and 48 percent of the workers. Similar proportions lacked some of the basic facilities of a comfortable working environment: for example one in five had no heating in winter and almost half could not adjust the lighting level. And nine percent reported that their work had interfered with their health. Most of these shortcomings were more commonly reported by manual workers, and it is likely therefore that the problems are less extensive than in more industrial areas, and becoming even less so as the composition of jobs in London shifts away from manual work. In other respects, however - such as the 43 percent lacking union representation in negotiating pay and conditions, the 39 percent without employers' pensions, or the 17 percent without full sick pay - conditions for London's service workers may not be significantly better. Overall the aspects of their job which many more people liked than disliked were its interest and the people with whom they worked, while promotion prospects were the one aspect of the job which more people disliked than liked. Pay, hours and conditions all attracted more positive than negative reactions while the balance of feelings about management and the use of their abilities was more or less neutral.

Several developments over the last decade, including the privatisation of work from local government and the health service, and the emphasis on 'flexible' employment practices, lead to the expectation that there will have been a substantial growth in the numbers working on short-term contracts or on a casual basis. In fact, however, while there has been some growth in these jobs in London they still represent only a very small part of London employment. In all, according to the 1989 LFS, some seven percent of the London work force were in temporary, casual or fixed-term appointments - and many of these were young professionals in fixed-term jobs which should lead to a secure career. A stronger cause for concern is the larger number involved in nominally permanent jobs with high turnover rates which reflect the lack of expectation on either side that the employment relation will be durable. These unstable jobs may be found in the bottom echelons of many organisations but are particularly common in construction and the private consumer services and in those remaining labour intensive industries facing intense competition from cheaper labour economies. In contrast to fixed-term white collar employment these are essentially 'dead-end' jobs with a high risk of spells of unemployment for the workers involved and little prospect of advancement to more secure or better rewarded opportunities

In these secondary sector jobs, according to the Greater London Living Standards Survey, about a quarter of the workers were entitled to less than a week's notice, while about half of them did not want to stay in their current jobs. Workers in this sector of employment tended to be less satisfied with most aspects of their job situation, the exceptions being in relation to the people they worked with (who were a stronger reason for liking *their* jobs) and the hours involved (with which they were as satisfied as others). Objective evidence from this source confirms that the unstable sector of employment also offers significantly lower pay to workers with (apparently) comparable characteristics and experience.


**Problems**

Massive de-industrialisation of the London economy, involving up to the early 1980s continuing decreases in employment, have caused a sense of loss in many quarters, leading to policy initiatives aimed at slowing or reversing this process (Young and Mills 1983). The restructuring of the economy, coupled with continuing decentralisation of the 'middle mass' of the population, has also had significant political implications in removing an important part of the traditional social basis of Labour politics in the city, notably a core of skilled (male) manual workers. The direction of change is not reversible, however, and as far as the real incomes of average Londoners are concerned the effect of lower employment levels and a transformed sectoral composition of activities appears to have been positive rather than negative. In the process the city's economic position may have become more exposed, with a greater dependence on one sector of activity (namely financial and business services), in which the Single European Market will open up more competition from rival centres than London has been used to. But among the factors which may have lowered the quality of life for the majority of the London population, the general performance of its economy does not figure prominently.

There are, however, major problems of a distributional nature, involving extensive economic deprivation and social divisions among the London population, which have probably been exacerbated by structural changes in the economy, as well as by essentially national factors. Among these economic problems we may include substantial poverty among a growing number of single-parent families, which is partly attributable to the low earnings levels of female workers (although the gender gap in pay is actually rather less in London than elsewhere). The two most critical problems for the 1990s, however, are the high levels of unemployment, especially among disadvantaged groups in the inner city, and the trend to a 're-casualisation' of the London labour market, particularly for those without formal education qualifications.

The numbers of people affected by unemployment substantially exceed the recorded unemployment 'rate', because of the continuing flow of individuals through this state (involving several times as many people within the course of, say, a year), because of 'hidden unemployment' among those discouraged from participation in the labour market (notably among women with children), and because of the insecurity felt by many whose jobs may be at risk. Of course not everybody faces equal risks, many are more or less immune (although the present recession has produced more than the usual number of white collar casualties), and the burden of unemployment is disproportionately borne by ethnic minorities, the young, the unqualified and those living in public sector housing. This narrows the base of concern about the issue, although providing some basis for politicians' fears that eventually (or occasionally) a sense of injustice may provoke substantial unrest, or unacceptable levels of crime. By any reasonable standards, however, the present levels of unemployment among those disadvantaged groups are unacceptably high.

Part of the reason for these high levels for Greater London, and the even higher rates recorded for inner east London, in particular, is the degree of spatial segregation within the functional London region, which concentrates the unemployed inside the core areas. It is not at all clear whether this spatial concentration of employment deprivation in itself constitutes a real problem, although it must increase political sensitivity to unemployment as an issue. Within a fixed overall level of unemployment, spatial concentrations only seem to matter in social and economic terms if there are significant externalities in terms of effects on motivation, communal support and access to information, and/or marked non-linearities in the relationship of local unemployment levels to social pathologies past some threshold level. We do not have substantial evidence on these relationships, but the general view is that spatial concentration of disadvantage is a 'bad thing'.

A second major problem is the 're-casualisation' of the London labour market - although this may be a rather extreme characterisation of the growing dependence of the unqualified (and some other weakly placed groups) on sets of 'secondary' jobs, with high rates of employment turnover, extensive rather than intensive personnel practices, and little prospect of occupational advancement. The allusion to casual employment, which in a strict sense still exists only on a rather small scale, should be a useful reminder, however, of how the inner London labour market operated before the entry of substantial factories at the turn of the century. Then, as now, a lack of stability in employment relations was associated with an economy characterised by small firms operating in highly competitive markets, and the potential, offered by the large metropolitan labour market, for firms (and workers) to rely on new labour (and jobs) being available when required. In these circumstances the external labour market clearly does provide a flexible substitute for the development of an internal force. Its potential limitations are three; there is likely to be under-investment in the personal development of the workers involved; these workers face risks, which they may not fully appreciate, of dropping down into 'careers' of intermittent unemployment (or 'under-employment'); and young workers, in particular, miss the processes of socialisation and integration afforded by more disciplined workplaces, union organisations and work-based co-operation and social interaction. At the level of local communities, social life, attitudes to education and so on might be expected to be quite different where a substantial proportion of the population is involved in such insecure employment. Good contemporary evidence on the causal connections with 'inner-city' social problems is lacking, but there is suggestive evidence from the late Victorian era linking the casual poor with ignorance, inarticulacy and disorganisation, together with "a hatred of the forces of law and order, a primitive and sometimes predatory hostility to the rich, a strong distaste for the 'cant' of the preachers and a willingness to resort to riot" (Jones 1971: 342). Moreover, the gradual attrition of this group as the London labour market stabilised was accompanied (over the period 1880 to 1950) by a sharp fall in London crime rates, both absolutely and relative to the rest of the country; with the onset of de-industrialisation after the late 1950s both trends went into sharp reverse (Gurr *et al* 1977: 111 and 159).[4]

Even the quality of race relations is liable to differ. Drawing on Bourgois' (1991) study of youths in Spanish Harlem, Duster (1993) argues that low-paying entry-level service jobs produce a level of emotional antagonism toward 'straight society' on their part which is quite different from both the 'oppositional culture' of defiance and resistance in factory work and the despair of those laid off from the industrial sector. In part this is because the service jobs required more of a subordination of the youths' own styles to the culture of their supervisors, and in part because their class-race anger is not mediated through a union or any other form of collective resistance. In the New York context the main alternative is involvement in the street-level drug trade, with a high risk of subsequent incarceration. But Duster argues that the situation and response of young Black Americans (and their European counterparts) is a harbinger of what is on the horizon for many others of the young, inexperienced and unskilled if whole new job structure and career ladders are not created.

## Diagnoses of the problems

There are four main hypotheses about the basis of these problems. The first, particularly current in the late 1970s and early 1980s traced their origin to what was perceived as a severe, cumulative and perhaps irreversible decline in the London economy, as evidenced particularly in the loss of half a million jobs between 1971 and 1984 (from a base of four million, already depleted by job losses right through the 1960s). This was the key perception underlying the new phase of national inner-city policy introduced by Peter Shore, then Secretary of State for the Environment, in 1976. Since then, however, employment levels have more or less stabilised, and the majority of forecasts envisage actual growth over the next decade (for example, Gordon 1990). Urban revival, evident also through most of the 1980s in New York City as in a number of other metropolitan areas, does not, however, seem to have removed many of the inner-city employment problems. These are clearly not related in any simple way to overall growth or decline in the urban economy. Nor would this be expected by anyone who looked back to the acute labour market problems evident, especially in the East End in London's late Victorian era of rapid growth (Jones 1971).

One reason for the lack of improvement is that it is the relationship between rates of growth in labour supply and in labour demand, rather than simply the rate of growth in jobs, which affects residents' chances of successful employment. The 1960s and at least the first half of the 1970s were a period of large-scale decentralisation of *both* population and employment from the urban core, two processes linked by a common pursuit of lower densities of occupation which largely cancelled each other out in terms of labour market effects.

To put the point baldly, there was no crisis of the London economy during these decades (merely a spatial rearrangement over an extended region), and the changes which did occur were not the cause of the (very real) employment problems of inner-city residents. In terms of relativities at least, these problems pre-dated the period of substantial contraction in London jobs, while in absolute terms their sharpest expression came (during the mid 1980s) when that contraction had come to a halt.

A second diagnosis focuses on the question of employment mismatch consequent on the particularly rapid shift of employment out of manual jobs in manufacturing and transport/wholesaling activities (which together lost 0.8 million jobs in London between 1971 and 1989 from a base of under 2 million) and the concentration of all employment growth in white collar financial and business services.

These represent an exaggerated version of broader trends in a de-industrialising British economy, with an impact on the likely balance between the supply and demand for less skilled labour which is exacerbated in London by the continuing social selectivity of out-migration from the city. Their general impact has been cushioned to a large extent by the long-term rise in educational standards which brings into the labour market in every area cohorts of new entrants much better equipped for higher level occupations than those in the retiring generation which they replace. At the national level this inter-generational upgrading of supply may be sufficient to match the rising demands of a changing educational structure, but that is unlikely to be equally true in London where the occupational restructuring has been proceeding so much faster. And, as we have already noted, unemployment rates in the city are very much higher among the unskilled and unqualified (although given *some* degree of skill or qualification its level appears quite irrelevant). Moreover, the margin of disadvantage among the unqualified does appear to be substantially greater in London than in other areas where the shift towards white collar employment has been slower (Buck and Gordon 1987).

The London labour force is actually a rather well qualified one, with 27 percent of resident workers in 1990 possessing a degree or other higher education qualification, against 16 percent nationally - and only 23 percent lacking any qualification, against 27 percent. But this is largely the consequence of the city's long-standing attraction for able young people from other areas. London's own school-leavers are less likely to achieve any graded results than most other areas of Britain, with 12.5 percent failing in this regard, against 9.1 percent nationally in 1988/9 - only Strathclyde, South Wales and the West Midlands, West Yorkshire and Merseyside metropolitan counties doing worse, for reasons which have never been completely explained.

However, a recent official survey concluded that "the coexistence of high levels of both vacancies and unemployment in London cannot be explained primarily in terms of a mismatch between the skills and experience of unemployed people and the type of vacancies available" - nor in terms of unrealistic wage expectations (Meadows *et al* 1988: 4). Rather it found that "many unemployed people need to look more intensively and more effectively for work and that employers need to recognise that many unemployed people in London have the qualities they are looking for". In other words it represented a labour market failure. A third of the current vacancies were for jobs requiring no previous knowledge or experience; many of the unemployed appeared to have (or have had) the necessary skills for many other jobs; and most of the unemployed were seeking jobs of a kind which were on offer. There was, however, a dual problem with respect to those unemployed for six months or more; on the one hand they were failing to apply for many of the vacancies which London employers had recently filled; on the other hand employers (perhaps erroneously) perceived the longer-term unemployed as poorly motivated and badly prepared both for job interviews and for work, and were often unaware of the pool of these people available in their areas. Interestingly, it was employers in the (low unemployment) outer boroughs who were more likely to have had applications from the longer-term unemployed, perhaps because these firms had to make more efforts or compromises in order to recruit.

A third diagnosis emphasises the distributional nature of the employment problem, explaining highly unequal outcomes in terms of imperfect and discriminatory labour market practices which stereotype and marginalise significant groups of workers on the basis of their 'personal' characteristics and/or their employment histories. According to this hypothesis lack of educational or trade qualifications disadvantages workers in much the same way that belonging to some ethnic minorities, being old, young, or a single man, or living in a council house do, namely in lowering their position in the 'queue' for jobs. The point is not that those falling in any of these categories *are unemployable* in the context of the present set of occupational requirements, but that, when employers have a choice, these groups are less likely to be given access to any given set of jobs. The problem is thus one of relative competitive positions, rather than of absolute deficiencies in required characteristics. The Meadows *et al* results lend support to this view, as does the fact that unemployment differentials always narrow when the labour market picks up (Meadows *et al* 1988).

A final diagnosis accounts for current problems in terms of a re-structuring of labour markets which has increasingly polarised employment opportunities, particularly in terms of the security which they afford and its relation to the possession of formal educational qualifications. The loss of industrial and transport jobs in London, followed by a halt to public sector growth, has curtailed the channels through which working-class youngsters without educational qualifications could gain access to reasonably stable jobs with a prospect of occupational advancement. For this group, largely shut out of the booming producer services, there has been an increased dependency on jobs in private consumer services where often highly competitive market conditions and unstable demands discourage the creation of jobs with any substantial tenure expectations. In London particularly, with its large and dynamic labour market, employers in these trades expect to meet their employment needs readily by external recruitment and do not give a high priority to reducing turnover.

Those working in these competitive and unstable industrial sectors are substantially more likely to become unemployed. Exposure to this instability is also a reason why those last working in unskilled (or unclassifiable) manual occupations are disproportionately unemployed. For both, the argument runs, it is the *job* which disadvantages (both directly and through the stigmatising marks which it leaves in a work history) rather than characteristics of the workers themselves. Training the workers may not help greatly therefore unless employment conditions change, or an upgrading of employment squeezes these jobs out.

Each of these London-focused diagnoses takes as given the state of the national labour market. In fact, however, developments in the national economy since the late 1970s are the main contributory factor to the scale of current labour market problems in London. In particular, it has been shown that the high levels of unemployment experienced in London over most of the past decade are predominantly the result of job losses elsewhere in the country, rather than anything happening to the London economy (Buck *et al* 1986; Gordon 1988). Because of strong migrational linkages to other regions, fluctuations in London unemployment tend to closely parallel those in the national total. Thus during the 1960s and 1970s when London employment was contracting sharply, unemployment in the city never rose above what now appears the quite modest national average - whereas in the 1980s as London's employment decline slowed and even reversed the city's unemployment was drawn upwards in the wake of collapsing employment in the industrial regions.

High levels of national unemployment brought high levels of unemployment to London, and the latter acted to exaggerate a series of long-standing inequalities and sources of disadvantage within London labour markets. As far as unemployment is concerned many of these inequalities appear to be proportional in character - for example council tenants are about twice as likely to be unemployed as owner-occupiers at any given level of unemployment - hence when total unemployment rises the extent of the gaps is magnified. In some cases the effect may be even stronger, because a slack labour market gives employers the scope to pursue their prejudices more fully than when they have to consider any available source of scarce labour.

To the London-specific diagnoses of the problem we have therefore to add the rival explanations of persistently high levels of national unemployment. These include, at the Keynesian end of the spectrum, accounts focused on the relative priority which national government policy has given to the control of inflation rather than to the maintenance of high levels of (particularly industrial) production. Other accounts, however, have emphasised the fact that the level of unemployment required to control inflation seems to have risen sharply since the 1970s, reducing the scope for such a switch of policy priorities, and pointing to some underlying source of inefficiency in the operation of the labour market (Layard *et al* 1991). Whether that is because, on the one hand, some residue of union power or a growing culture of dependency interferes with competitive processes or on the other, because continuing high unemployment has served to shut out the long-term unemployed and some others from effective participation in the market, is also contested however. Any of this last set of diagnoses has implications, albeit contradictory, for action at a city level, in order to impact on *national* unemployment.

## Policy initiatives

During the past decade of predominantly high unemployment a wide variety of policy initiatives have been pursued on employment issues in London by various central government agencies, by the London boroughs and (while it existed) by the Greater London Council (GLC). Almost none of these, however, were on a scale which could have been expected to have a substantial impact on the level of unemployment in the city. The sole exception could be the major investment programme initiated by the London Docklands Development Corporation (LDDC), which has spent about £1 billion since 1981, although only a small fraction of the expected employment creation (amounting to 200,000 jobs) has yet materialised.

Despite its controversial origins as an independent agency imposed on Labour or Alliance-controlled London boroughs by a Conservative central government, the LDDC strategy for the inner east London labour market had a basic commonality with much of the activity of boroughs and of the GLC in focusing on job creation as the essential ingredient. This reflects the first of the diagnoses discussed in the previous section, which traces the origins of the employment problem to chronic net job loss in the London economy.

The basic limitation of this approach is that there is no guarantee that the additional jobs will accrue to London residents, still less to any of the disadvantaged groups, or those living in the high unemployment areas in the immediate vicinity of Docklands. Time series evidence on past employment and unemployment trends indicates that marginal jobs in London have a weak effect on unemployment levels (except in the case of job losses through redundancy), with the bulk of the impact leaking out through adjustments in migration and commuting patterns (Gordon 1988). For service sector jobs, which are the most likely source of policy-induced employment, there has been *no* detectable effect on London unemployment. The weak link between job creation and unemployment reflects the combination of two factors. First is the openness of the London labour market (like most urban labour markets), particularly to cross-border commuting. Second there is the relatively weak competitive position of many of those represented among the London unemployed, which means that in-commuters or in-migrants to the city will often be preferred. Where new jobs are actually filled by an already-employed Londoner, the consequent vacancy chain is much more likely to end with recruitment of somebody from outside the city than with an unemployed Londoner gaining a job. Both factors are likely to operate particularly strongly for white collar service jobs which attract migrants and commuters over long distances, and which are less likely to be open to disadvantaged groups.

Major ideological differences have been reflected in the *means* used by Conservative central government and Labour local authorities to promote employment growth in London - and even more in the rhetoric used to justify and draw wider, national lessons from their policies.[5] The former Greater London Council's *London Labour Plan* developed a 'productionist' strategy for the London labour market, as an alternative to what it identified as monetarist and Keynesian approaches (Greater London Council 1986). This took a very wide view of the concerns of a labour market policy, including not only issues of wages and employment, but also the quality of work, its organisation, private time, the needs of domestic workers and issues of gender roles, contracts, collective bargaining and economic democracy. Developing the concept of 'restructuring for labour' introduced in their *London Industrial Strategy* it saw a clear scope (and need) for industrial intervention to promote strategic restructuring at a sectoral level in order to assist productivity growth (rather than simple cost-cutting), while protecting the human needs of workers and actively developing their skills (rather than encouraging de-skilling) (Greater London Council 1985). Another major concern was with overcoming divisions in the workforce, between the position of predominantly white male permanent full-time workers in the organised 'core' jobs and the 'periphery' of fragmented, less skilled, insecure and lower paid secondary jobs occupied particularly by women, black people and migrant workers.

The extensive portfolio of policies outlined in the *Plan* went beyond job creation and job saving, to include action on equal opportunities, training, contract compliance, resistance to privatisation, enterprise planning, and (at the national level) minimum wage levels and social security. However, job creation was seen as a fundamental requirement. The basic perspective was that of the London economy as a whole. A case was recognised for area labour market policies geared to local pools of specialised skilled labour and local political or union structures. However, the *Plan* recognised that the employment problems of residents in particular inner-city areas resulted from wider economic forces, combined with the impact of employment discrimination on disadvantaged groups in their populations, rather than from the failure of local economies. To this extent its prescriptions were less localist than those of individual boroughs whose actions to create or preserve employment have always been liable to involve a large element of displacement of jobs from other areas within London.

Local authorities in their direct interventions and the Greater London Enterprise Board (GLEB) implementing the former GLC's industrial strategy have been concerned not only with new employment generation but also with job saving. For private sector jobs this is a risky operation involving hard commercial judgements, which public officials have had little experience in making, often in pressurised crisis situations. On the other hand there is little doubt that success in job saving would be more valuable than job creation, in terms of the job-for-job impact on unemployment, particularly *within* the urban area involved. Job saving, when it can be achieved, normally has a direct impact on unemployment levels within an area, whereas the main effects of job creation commonly accrue to commuters and in-migrants from other areas - and may never lead to the re-employment of a substantial proportion of redundant workers (Gordon 1988). To pursue a cost-effective job saving strategy, which does more than marginally extend the life of a set of jobs, requires, however, staff expertise and a long-term approach to the problems of a sector, which cannot effectively be sustained by local authorities operating at a borough level within London. (In some cases short-term assistance from boroughs seems actually to have exacerbated eventual job losses by encouraging an over-optimistic stance on the part of managers in uncompetitive firms.) Until abolition of the GLC effectively terminated its operations, the GLEB's sectoral planning did, however, provide the basis for a more hard-headed approach to job saving across London as a whole. Its overall budget for all its activities was around £30 million per annum; in the first 17 months of its operations approved investment amounting to £8.2 million was supposed to have led to 2000 additional jobs (Mawson and Miller 1987) - that is about £4000 per job - although like all these project related assessments this takes no account of displacement effects.

Conservative initiatives in London have also used the language of 'enterprise' in pursuing job creation, although in their case the role of government is supposed to be supportive rather than directional. Two versions of this approach have both been implemented in the former London Docklands, an 'enterprise zone' with restricted government activity within it, and a Development Corporation providing the infrastructural support for physical regeneration. Of these two overlapping initiatives, the Isle of Dogs Enterprise Zone has seen a growth of 9000 jobs between its designation in 1982 and the end of 1989. Over this period there was a total public sector investment in the Zone of £85 million in land acquisition and infrastructure provision, while the level of rate revenue foregone was running at £8 million per annum in 1988-89 (Central Statistical Office 1991). In addition tax expenditure is involved in the provision of 100 percent capital allowances. A significant number job gains have therefore been secured, possibly at the expense of other areas in London, at a cost of £10,000 plus per job. Over the wider area covered by the LDDC, between its establishment in 1981 and 1989 some 28,000 jobs were attracted, of which over three quarters are estimated to have transferred from elsewhere (Docklands Forum and Birkbeck College (DFBC) 1990). The net gain to London as a result of regeneration is less than this implies because many of these 'new jobs' would have gone to another site in the city in the absence of Docklands development, while some of the 13,000 jobs lost to the area over this period will have been displaced as a result of the regeneration process. Particularly since substantial office space is now materialising elsewhere in central London, it actually seems unlikely that London as a whole has gained *any* extra employment as a result of this regeneration. There *has*, however, clearly been a shift of employment growth into inner east London, an area of previously poor employment performance and continuing high unemployment. But relative unemployment rates in this part of the city have generally deteriorated during the 1980s, implying that local residents have not benefited. An apparent exception is the immediate Tower Hamlets district, but what has happened there is that the attraction of a substantial number of new middle class residents has lowered the proportion of unemployed in the population without reducing their numbers.

Apart from job creation and job saving the other two main strands of policy prescription for London employment have involved education/training and equal opportunities policy. Of these, training has been the most widely advocated and called forth the most initiatives, although the effectiveness, and even the seriousness, of many of these have been severely questioned. Three sets of objectives for training policy should be distinguished: to improve the productivity of the labour force, enhancing competitiveness, growth and wealth creation; to occupy those who would otherwise be unemployed, or dropped out of the formal labour force; and to improve the competitive position of the unemployed or other disadvantaged groups within the labour market. Criticism of mainstream 'training' programmes initiated by central government has hinged largely on the question as to whether it actually serves the last of these objectives. In particular the issues are whether there has been any effective targeting of disadvantaged groups (or a reproduction of employers' conventional stereotypes) and whether the 'training' provided for them is designed to significantly improve their competitive position.

In relation to education the basic problems are the substantial proportion of Londoners (particularly in inner east London - the old Inner London Education Authority (ILEA) divisions 3-5 and 8-9) leaving school without formal qualifications, and the diminished chances (particularly for males) in this position of achieving occupational qualifications, secure employment with prospects for advancement, and a recognition of their personal abilities, in the context of the more polarised labour market of the 1990s. The most important initiative to address these problems has been the East London Compact, based on a model imported from Boston, Massachusetts by the former ILEA in conjunction with the London Enterprise Agency in 1987. The aim of the Compact was to improve the linkage between schools and employers in the area by setting and documenting standards of achievement for all children, which if met would guarantee at least a job interview. Early monitoring by ILEA of the Compact's progress suggests that despite a raising of awareness, immediate achievements in terms of pupil placement with local firms have been limited, since most of those achieving the prescribed standards then proceeded to stay on at school (DFBC 1991). The Compact may not yet have hit the right target but, in focusing on the need to motivate pupils with a realistic prospect of rewards in the labour market, and to provide credible documentation of the job-related abilities of a wider range of school leavers, its strategy appears to be the right one.

Equal opportunities policies attempt first, to redress direct and indirect discrimination in the operation of recruitment, training and promotion procedures, and second, to develop the aspirations of groups traditionally disadvantaged by such discrimination. The aim is thus to improve both the efficiency and the equity of the London labour market. Labour authorities in London, including the former GLC, developed strong equal opportunities platforms during the 1980s in recognition of the changing composition of the city's working-class electorate. Policy focused both on the improvement of performance within local authorities themselves, to the point where they could be regarded as 'model employers', and on the use of contract compliance requirements to influence behaviour among their suppliers. No overall assessment of the impact of these policies is yet available, however.

**Some issues for investigation**

The 1980s saw both an end to the long process of employment decline in London and a growing polarisation of incomes and employment opportunities in the city. This polarisation reflects a combination of very high levels of national unemployment - mitigated in the late 1980s but returning now - with continuing structures of social disadvantage and the loss of many of the more secure career opportunities available to the educationally unqualified. In the face of de-industrialisation, London's enhanced status as a global city and centre of fashionable consumption, and a new emphasis on economic 'flexibility', London's employment structure was reverting to its pre-twentieth century small firm based service economy.

In the face of these changes, as well as some ideological pressures, there has been a renewal of concern about the role of an 'urban underclass', similar to that identified in US cities, or for that matter in Victorian London. Discussion of this issue has, however, been fraught both by strong ideological preconceptions as to the nature and role of this 'class', and by substantial ambiguities as to who it is comprised of. As with earlier debates about the 'culture of poverty' it has also been unclear whether the underclass is identifiable essentially as the victims of processes of marginalisation, or by attitudes and behavioural tendencies which potentially threaten those in mainstream society. Heath has shown that for one conceptualisation of the underclass (as those more or less permanently excluded from the labour market) there is no general evidence of their supposedly anti-social values in relation to family, work or their economic responsibilities (Heath 1991). However, there may be other conceptualisations of the underclass for which this is not the case.

The category considered by Heath (together with his colleagues in the Policy Studies Institute seminar) included two major groups within the working-age population, namely the long-term unemployed and economically inactive single parents. It could also include the counterparts to a New York type underclass of individuals working in the informal/criminal economies, but this appears to be confined to single people who have withdrawn from the formal labour market (a very small category in the UK, although a little more significant in inner London). In addition to these, however, a further, somewhat marginalised group is comprised of those in insecure, secondary employment, lacking a permanent attachment to the labour market, rather than being permanently excluded from it. It is within this group - and the jobs employing them - that we may find the closest counterpart to the Victorian underclass. And it is in the context of an ample supply of dead-end jobs offering a living wage but no prospect of gain from long-term job attachment that we might expect to find present-centred, individualistic values, lack of interest in human capital formation and a lack of commitment to other social relations. Whether any of this is true or not is a question well worth investigating.

A second important question relates to the course of ethnic inequalities during the 1980s. The importance of these inequalities in the labour market, and the extent to which they reflect discrimination have become clearer during the decade - but so has their unevenness, as more disaggregated ethnic categories come to be considered. Indians are clearly doing quite well in the London labour market (and in school) - so apparently are the 'black British', whoever they may be[6] - but Afro-Caribbeans and Bangladeshis are not. During the recovery phase of the late 1980s unemployment data suggested that ethnic differentials were being substantially narrowed. Whether this is a purely temporary phenomenon, in what areas of employment minorities have been making progress, and what the implications are of economic success among the 'black British' are important questions to address.

An understanding of the evolving form of ethnic inequality in the labour market is important not only for its own sake, but because it may provide a model for analysing other, less visible class-related forms of disadvantage in the labour market. Another avenue of approach to this (also of great significance for inner London) would be to try to explain why it is that, after many other variables have been controlled for, public sector tenants in London (as elsewhere) remain twice as liable as owner-occupiers to experience unemployment. This is one of the major causes of areal concentrations of unemployment, but to assess its significance we also need some more direct evidence as to whether spatially concentrated unemployment is actually worse in social or economic terms than an even dispersal of the misery.

A final issue, of direct importance to a wider cross-section of the London population, is that of the quality of life enjoyed by those responsible for public services in London (relative to their peers elsewhere), its implications for the quality of service provision in the city, and thereby for the quality of life of all London residents.

**Directions for policy**

To improve and maintain the quality of life for Londoners there are four key policy issues needing attention in the first half of the 1990s: first, maintenance of London's competitive position as a high-level service centre against the new challenges it faces in the Single European Market (SEM). In effect the SEM means the end of London's monopoly position in a national market, exposing it to the same competitive forces which have wrought New York's much more unstable economic history in recent times. To compete successfully with Paris, Frankfurt, Berlin, the Randstad *et al* will require the coherent and effective strategic planning of the whole London region which it currently lacks. This will need to provide an efficient system of personal transportation, linked to the development of sub-regional employment centres, the decentralisation of activities for which a central location is less vital, and to develop a competitive economic strategy for the city. The loss of the Greater London authority must now be treated as an opportunity to create an executive planning agency for a 'Still Greater London' region with indirect representation of both local electors and business. Social as well as economic planning should be within its remit, in view of the critical need to avert social conflict within the city on a scale undermining its competitive prospects.

Second, to this end, and to ensure that all Londoners benefit from economic success in the future, there is a crucial need to re-integrate economically disadvantaged groups including ethnic minorities by a more energetic attack on all forms of discrimination in the labour market. The lead here must come from public sector employers, and a pre-requisite for success will be the continued availability of public sector jobs. A complementary approach, advocated by Buck *et al* (1986), Hall (1989) and by the Lambeth Inner Area Study a decade earlier (Shankland *et al* 1977), is to make it easier than it has been for unskilled workers and low-income households to move out of London. This ran counter to the former GLC's planning strategy and has not been adopted into policy. As conceived by Buck *et al* the aim would be to encourage a decentralisation of labour supply at the bottom end of the labour market to parallel that which has long been proceeding among white collar groups and skilled manual workers, but has been blocked for those with insufficient incomes to gain access to owner-occupation. To achieve this would require the construction of low-income housing close enough to the city to make commuting back to existing workplaces feasible in the early stages, even for those on low incomes, and associated with new employment which would allow a subsequent switch to out-of-town workplaces.

The third issue is the reversal of the shift towards a more casualised labour market, both through educational/training initiatives to reduce the unqualified segment of the labour force, and the pursuit of minimum employment standards in all firms receiving assistance from public organisations.

The fourth key issue is the financial flexibility for local authorities and other public sector employers to ensure recruitment of staff of the quality required to deliver adequate, efficient and competitive public services for London residents and businesses. A high level of such public service provision must be recognised as an indispensable element for the sustainability of economic success in a great city such as London.

## Notes

1. These are residence-based estimates of the proportion of economically active people actively seeking work, based on an update of the 1989 Labour Force Survey.
2. Published unemployment rates for London relate the level of unemployment among residents to those defined as economically active in the city on a workplace basis, rather than to the smaller number actually resident there. Consequently they understate the true incidence of unemployment among the latter group. Estimates in this paper are adjusted to a residence basis.
3. Details of this survey are provided in Townsend *et al* (1987), although the figures cited here derive from unpublished tabulations from a data tape made available by Peter Townsend.
4. For New York evidence on the link between crime and casual employment see McGahey (1986).
5. In their comparative study of Labour authorities' local economic development policies including that of the GLC, Mawson and Miller stress that "interventionist authorities

recognise that they can have little more than a marginal impact on the problems facing their areas .... they wish to show that it is possible to develop cost-effective initiatives .... which also serve an exemplary purpose in suggesting that, if similar approaches were introduced at national and regional levels, then a solution to the present economic malaise would be found" (Mawson and Miller 1987: 145). Similarly it is clear that Enterprise Zones were intended (by the Thatcher administration) as symbolic action to make an ideological point about the potential for releasing 'enterprise' from the fetters of government control on a much wider scale than the few small areas given EZ status. Docklands development, although a much more substantial commitment, also has symbolic significance both for national policy and for London.

6.     The Greater London Living Standards Survey provides this tantalising piece of evidence (Townsend *et al* 1987). Using self-ascribed ethnic categories, including 'black British' as well as more specific ethnic origins, it shows that this first group, who from their residential distribution are inferred to be about 90 percent Afro-Caribbean and 10 percent Indian, had unemployment rates very similar to those of the white population. Multivariate analysis shows that their unemployment rate was substantially below that of those identified as Afro-Caribbean even when differences in education, age and marital status are controlled for. It is not clear, however, whether the choice of this identity has causal significance in relation to labour market success or is influenced by a more favourable experience in the labour market.

## References

Bourgois P (1991) In search of respect: the new service economy and the crack alternative in Spanish Harlem, Working Paper No 21, New York: Russell Sage Foundation.

Buck N H (1991) Social polarisation in the inner city: an analysis of the impact of labour market and household change, in Cross M and Payne G (eds) *Social Inequality and the Enterprise Culture*, London: Falmer Press.

Buck N H and Fainstein N (1992) A comparative history 1880-1973, in Fainstein S S, Gordon I R and Harloe M (eds) *Divided Cities: New York and London in the contemporary world*, Oxford: Blackwell.

Buck N H and Gordon I R (1987) The beneficiaries of employment growth: the experience of disadvantaged groups in expanding labour markets, in Hausner V (ed) *Critical Issues in Urban Economic Development Vol II*, Oxford: Clarendon Press.

Buck N H, Gordon I R and Young K G (1986) *The London Employment Problem*, Oxford: Clarendon Press.

Central Statistical Office (1991) *Regional Trends*, London: HMSO.

Cohen R B (1981) The new international division of labour multinational corporations and the urban hierarchy, in Dear M J and Scott A J (eds), *Urbanization, Urban Planning and Capitalist Society*, London: Methuen.

Docklands Forum and Birkbeck College (1990) *Employment in Docklands*, London: Docklands Forum.

Duster T (1993) Post-industrialism and youth unemployment: African-Americans as harbingers, in Lawson R, McFate K and Wilson W J (eds), *Poverty, Inequality and the Crisis of Social Policy*, New York: Sage.

Fainstein S S, Gordon I R and Harloe M (eds) (1992) *Divided Cities: New York and London in the contemporary world*, Oxford: Blackwell.

Fothergill S and Gudgin G (1982) *Unequal Growth*, London: Heinemann.

Friedmann J and Wolff G (1982) World city formation: an agenda for research and action, *International Journal of Urban and Regional Research* **6**, 309-44.

Gordon I R (1990) *The 1990 Round of Employment Forecasts for London*, London: London Planning Advisory Committee.

Gordon I R (1989) Urban unemployment, in Herbert D T and Smith D M (eds) *Social Problems and the City: new perspectives*, Oxford: Oxford University Press.

Gordon I R (1988) Evaluating the effect of employment change on local unemployment, *Regional Studies* **22**, 135-147.

Greater London Council (1986) *London Labour Plan*, London: GLC.

Greater London Council (1985) *London Industrial Strategy*, London: GLC.

Gurr T R, Grabosky P N and Hula R C (1977) *The Politics of Crime and Conflict: a comparative history of four cities*, London: Sage.

Hall P G (1989) *London 2001*, London: Unwin Hyman.

Heath A (1991) The attitudes of the underclass, paper presented to the conference on "The idea of an underclass in Britain", Policy Studies Institute, London (26 February).

Jones G S (1971) *Outcast London: A study of the relationship between classes in Victorian Society*, Oxford: Clarendon Press.

King A D (1990) *Global Cities: post-imperialism and the internationalization of London*, London: Routledge.

Layard R, Nickell S and Jackman R (1991) *Unemployment: macroeconomic performance and the labour market*, Oxford: Oxford University Press.

McGahey R M (1986) Economic conditions, neighbourhood organization and urban crime, in Reiss A J and Tonry M (eds) *Communities and Crime*, Chicago: University of Chicago Press.

Mawson J and Miller D (1987) Interventionist approaches in local employment and economic development: the experience of Labour local authorities, in Hausner V H (ed) *Critical Issues to Urban Economic Development Vol 1*, Oxford: Clarendon Press.

Meadows P, Cooper H and Bartholomew R (1988) *The London Labour Market*, London: HMSO.

Shankland G, Willmott P and Jordan D (1977) *Inner London, Policies for Dispersal and Balance*, London: HMSO.

Townsend P, Corrigan P and Kowazik U (1987) *Poverty and Labour in London*, London: Low Pay Unit.

Tyler P (1984) *Geographical Variations in Industrial Costs*, DP12, Cambridge: Dept of Land Economy.

Young K G and Mills L (1983) *Managing the Post-industrial City*, London: Heinemann.

# 3 Crime in London: an assessment

*Mike Hough and Pat Mayhew*

This paper sketches out the shape of crime problems facing London in the 1990s, and considers possible approaches to these problems. It uses survey findings and other statistics to outline: the extent of crime in London; comparisons with other parts of the country and abroad; crime trends; fear of crime; what public priorities are for dealing with crime; and attitudes to the police. The final part of the paper covers issues that could be tackled in the proposed survey of Londoners and New Yorkers.

## Crime in London - the shape of the problem

Assessing the shape of the crime problem in London necessarily involves comparisons. The ones most commonly made are comparisons over time - is the problem getting better or worse? One can also look to neighbouring regions or countries - is the problem any more marked than elsewhere? Then there are comparisons with other social problems - does problem A warrant more resources than problem B? Do people think that problem A is a more pressing one than problem B? The final part of the equation is the solubility of the problem. The more intractable it is, the less - according to some logics - it is actually a problem: a problem without a solution is not a problem at all.

Crime is notoriously hard to measure, and it is also very hard to say precisely what achieves any impact on it. Because crimes are not always reported to the police, and not always recorded by the police, and because only a small proportion of offences are dealt with by the courts, the statistics generated by the criminal justice system cannot be used with any reliability to answer these questions. They say as much about the operation of the system as they do about the problems of crime themselves. Wherever possible, therefore, this paper draws on survey data collected independently of the criminal justice process. In particular, it makes use of the *British Crime Survey* (BCS), three sweeps of which have now been carried out, in 1982, 1984 and 1988.[1] It also draws on the *International Crime Survey* (ICS), which compared victimisation in different countries in 1988.[2]

London's crime problem, as measured by the 1988 BCS, is predominantly one of property offences: 37 percent of incidents uncovered by the BCS are to do with motor vehicles, and 11 percent are burglaries. Only 6 percent are crimes of violence, and a further 10 percent assaults without injury.

Crime rates within London vary widely, and there is no doubt that levels of crime in parts of the city are several times higher than the average. Analysis by the ACORN typology of neighbourhoods shows that areas at particular risk are poor council estates, mixed inner city areas, and high status inner city areas (and this is the case elsewhere); those in a fourth ACORN category - modern family housing, also emerge as at risk of household crime, but not so much as elsewhere in the country.[3] Local crime surveys in some of the inner city boroughs have painted a similar picture of high risks in some areas (for example Jones *et al* 1986; London Borough of Newham 1987; Painter *et al* 1989).

There are several types of crime which the BCS cannot cover: shoplifting and other forms of theft against organisations and institutions, for example; commercial burglaries; vandalism to public property; and the so-called 'victimless crimes'. Crimes recorded in the Metropolitan Police District (MPD) in 1990 are listed in the Appendix to this chapter.

## Comparisons with the rest of England and Wales

Crime rates in London, in common with those of other large cities, are higher than in other parts of the country: in 1987, 14.6 percent of the adult population were Londoners, while 15.7 percent of crimes, as measured by the BCS, were committed there. Like the BCS, police statistics suggest that London compares not unfavourably with other conurbations. In 1990 it had the highest rates per head of population for violence, robbery and fraud (the latter no surprise, given its status as a commercial centre); but burglary rates were lower than in most other metropolitan forces, and figures for theft and criminal damage unexceptional. (Moreover, expressing crime in terms of rate per population inevitably shows London in a poor light, because the large non-resident population made up of office-workers, tourists and so on are omitted from the denominator.)

## International comparisons

At present, there are no strictly comparable data sets which enable crime in London to be compared with cities abroad. As yet, there are no survey data enabling this; and comparison of crime statistics recorded by police in different jurisdictions can be very misleading indeed, given differences not only in reporting and recording practices, but also in legal definitions. It is thus with some misgivings that we have included the figures in the table below. This shows levels of selected recorded offences in the MPD and New York City (similar in size at about seven million population), and in England and Wales, and the United States in general. The most striking - and well-known - comparison is for homicide: in 1989, New York's recorded homicide rate, excluding attempts, was ten times higher than London's. Taking murder, rape, serious assault and robbery together, New York's rate was some 3.4 times higher than London's. Theft of motor vehicles was twice as high, although burglary was lower in New York. (The picture is different for the countries as a whole respectively: violent crime was about 1.6 times as high in the USA as in England and Wales, while both thefts of motor vehicles and burglary were lower in the USA.)

**Table 1**

**Recorded offences per 100,000 population in the
Metropolitan Police District and New York City, 1989**

|  | MPD | New York | England and Wales | USA |
|---|---|---|---|---|
| Homicide | 2.4 | 25.9 | 1.3 | 8.7 |
| Rape | 12.3 | 44.2 | 6.6 | 38.1 |
| Serious Assault | 420.5 | 962.8 | 340.9 | 383.4 |
| Robbery | 238.5 | 1267.2 | 65.8 | 233.0 |
| Theft of Motor Vehicles | 921.4 | 1816.5 | 780.7 | 630.4 |
| Burglary | 2078.4 | 1646.4 | 1639.0 | 1276.3 |
| Violent crime[1] | 673.8 | 2300.0 | 414.5 | 663.1 |
| Total | 3673.6 | 5762.9 | 2834.1 | 2569.7 |

Source: For the Metropolitan Police District - Report for the Commissioner of the Police of the Metropolis, 1989 (London: Metropolitan Police, 1990); for England and Wales - Criminal Statistics, England and Wales, 1989 (London: HMSO, 1990); for New York and the USA - Uniform Crime Reports, 1989 (Washington: US Department of Justice, 1990).

1 Violence: homicide, rape, serious assault and robbery.

Although we cannot compare survey data for London and New York, the results of the 1988 ICS provide some useful background against which to judge the above figures. The data from the ICS must itself be interpreted with care, because telephone ownership varied between country, as did response rates to the survey among those who were contacted; and the small sample sizes inevitably yielded imprecise estimates of crime rates. (The samples are too small to enable analysis by type of area within each country.)

Nonetheless the results are of great interest. Overall crime rates in England and Wales in 1988 were lower than in the United States, and were also below the European average. Rates of car theft in England and Wales, however, are higher than in the United States and in most European countries. In contrast to the picture from recorded offences, the ICS shows burglary to be more common in the USA.


## Crime trends

There can be no doubt that crime has risen rapidly in London since the war. Statistics of crime recorded by the police provide the only long-term information on trends, and these again must be interpreted with care. The means of reporting crimes to the police have improved over time (notably with the introduction of the telephone); computerised statistical systems make it easier to record crime; and, arguably, the logic of resource bargaining gives the police an enduring incentive to increase recording levels. The BCS has demonstrated that police statistics have overstated the increase in crime between 1981 and 1987 in England and Wales as a whole and the same may be true for both the preceding and following periods.

However, the sheer scale of the increase in recorded crime since the war makes it inconceivable that crime rates have stood still. Fifty years ago the Metropolitan Police recorded 100,000 crimes per year; 30 years ago the figure had doubled to 200,000, by the 1980s it had risen to 600,000, and it now stands at 900,000 offences per year. Even so, the rise in recorded crime in London between 1981 and 1991 was much shallower than for England and Wales as a whole: 47 percent as against 78 percent. And indeed the rise in crime in London was less steep than in most other metropolitan forces. Trends in recorded crime in London - as distinct from recorded crime levels - were less favourable over the 1980s than New York's. Between 1980 and 1989, recorded crime in New York dropped by about 12 percent (in parallel with an overall drop in the USA largely mirrored by the US National Crime Survey trend); in London there was a 10 percent increase.

Time horizons in assessing social problems are usually measured in decades, and rarely exceed 50 years; but it is worth taking a longer view. It is clear from sources such as Samuel Pepys' diary that three centuries ago, a person of any wealth was ill-advised to venture out across London after dark without armed servants. The writings of reformers such as Henry Fielding and John Colquhoun a century or so later paint a picture of metropolitan life where violence and predatory crime were commonplace. The sheer volume of Victorian crime prevention 'hardware' - locks, bolts, bars and grills - which is still evident throughout London demonstrates eloquently that London was by no means crime-free a century ago.

## Public disorder

Large-scale disorder and riot has intermittently occurred both in London and in conurbations elsewhere in the country for centuries. The very rarity of these events makes it hard to detect any significant trend. One can point to: the disorders in London associated with the suffragette movement at the start of the century; the riots associated with demobilisation at the end of the First World War; a long series of disorders linked to unemployment in the 1920s and 1930s; and racial disturbances in the 1950s. The 1980s saw several occurrences of serious large-scale disorder in London, starting with the Brixton riots in 1981. A common element to many of these was the hostility towards the police of young men from ethnic minority groups, especially those of West Indian origin. To date in the 1990s, there have been riots associated with the community charge and a number of smaller-scale disorders with somewhat more hedonistic and materialistic origins.

Putting these incidents in some sort of context, London's experience is certainly not unique in Britain. There have been similar incidents in other cities, and even in towns previously taken to be icons of tranquillity. Clearly London has a special vulnerability as a capital city and as a political centre, but it would be wrong to conceive of it as a 'riot capital'.

## Public concerns about crime

Another approach to defining the shape and size of the crime problem facing Londoners is to ask them. The BCS has included a number of relevant questions. Thus, in 1988, 28 percent of Londoners thought that their area had higher crime rates than the rest of the country; this was substantially higher than the national figure (15 percent), though only slightly higher than the 22 percent in other conurbations. Respondents were also asked whether a selection of 'incivilities', such as noisy neighbours, drunks, tramps, rubbish, litter and vandalism, were common in their area. There was no consistent difference to emerge between London and other conurbations, though not surprisingly such problems were generally rated as less common outside cities. Although the information is now somewhat dated, the 1984 BCS can also provide some relevant information: 11 percent of Londoners cited crime and vandalism as the worst problem in their area, compared with 8 percent in other conurbations and 2 percent elsewhere; 6 percent cited incivilities and bad neighbours, compared with 13 percent in other cities and 7 percent elsewhere. To provide some context, 28 percent of Londoners said that there was nothing wrong with their area, 15 percent complained about traffic, and 9 percent mentioned the lack of amenities and shops.

The British Crime Survey shows that fear of crime in London is higher than in the country as a whole, but roughly comparable to other British cities. The table below shows that more women in London feel unsafe on the streets than in other cities; but anxiety about a range of property crimes is lower. As in other cities, a minority of people can be identified on whose quality of life fear of crime has a deeply dislocating effect. This includes people who live in high-crime areas, the physically vulnerable and those who are socially isolated; groups such as the elderly poor, who are often frail and tend to live in isolation in high crime areas, are especially susceptible. The key policy issue here is the extent to which the anxiety is an informed response to high levels of risk, or the consequence of misunderstandings, misperceptions and media exaggerations.

**Table 2**

**Concern about crime in London**

|  | Metropolitan Police District | Other metropolitan areas[1] | Other areas[1] | All areas |
|---|---|---|---|---|
| % feeling very unsafe after dark |  |  |  |  |
| Women | 27 | 24 | 16 | 19 |
| Age 60 or over | 28 | 27 | 17 | 21 |
| % very worried about |  |  |  |  |
| Burglary | 23 | 27 | 15 | 19 |
| Mugging | 24 | 27 | 16 | 20 |
| Theft from car[2] | 19 | 26 | 13 | 17 |
| Theft of car[2] | 21 | 31 | 16 | 20 |
| Unweighted N (all respondents) | 1,485 | 3,131 | 5,738 | 10,353 |

Source:  1988 British Crime Survey (weighted data).

1  "Other metropolitan areas" and "Other areas" relate to England and Wales.

2  Worry about thefts of and from cars based on car owners.

Local crime surveys have provided some useful information about policing priorities as perceived by the London public. For example, the first and second Islington Crime Surveys (Crawford *et al* 1990) asked respondents to select from 20 crimes those three on which they felt the police should spend more time. The ordering of the most commonly selected crimes in 1988 was: sexual assault; street robbery; burglary; child abuse; sale of drugs; drunken driving; vandalism; and racial attacks.

**Attitudes to the police**

The 1988 BCS shows that Londoners rate local police performance slightly less favourably than people elsewhere, but their assessment is, if anything, more favourable than that of other big-city residents; see the table below. In London and elsewhere, ethnic minorities are less likely than whites to feel that the police are performing well, even if they are slightly more likely than whites to think that their local police are better than elsewhere. A further worrying finding is that ratings of the police tend to be lower among those with most contact, even where this contact was solicited rather than imposed upon the respondent (compare with Skogan 1990).

Table 3

**Attitudes to the police in London**

| | Metropolitan Police District | Other metropolitan areas[1] | Other areas[1] | All areas |
|---|---|---|---|---|
| % feeling local police do a good job[2] | | | | |
| All respondents | 72 | 69 | 78 | 75 |
| Aged 30 yrs and under | 64 | 66 | 75 | 71 |
| Whites | 73 | 69 | 79 | 76 |
| Non-whites | 58 | 60 | 62 | 59 |
| % feeling local police do better job than elsewhere[2] | | | | |
| All respondents | 13 | 9 | 14 | 13 |
| Aged 30 yrs and under | 14 | 13 | 17 | 15 |
| Whites | 12 | 8 | 14 | 13 |
| Non-whites | 15 | 15 | 20 | 15 |
| Unweighted $N$ (all respondents) | 712 | 1,488 | 2,707 | 4,907 |

Source: 1988 British Crime Survey (weighted data).

1 "Other metropolitan areas" and "Other areas" relate to England and Wales.
2 Those who thought the police did a "fairly" or "very" good job.

In common with the rest of the country, ratings of the police fell over the 1980s, according to the BCS; and local surveys suggest that this decline is continuing. The police have made a very determined attempt to reverse the decline over the last few years, introducing a more explicit 'service orientation'. Future surveys of attitudes to the police, including the 1992 BCS, will indicate whether this has been successful.

## Crime in London: a summary

In making sense of the various sources of information presented here, there is a difficult tightrope to walk between complacency and alarmism. On the one hand, crime in London does not appear to be significantly worse than in other large cities in England and Wales and, by extension, than in Europe; it is fairly certain that its overall crime rate, and especially the violent crime rate, is much lower than New York's. There is also some evidence to suggest that the rise in crime in London has been shallower than in other parts of the country.  On the other hand, the fact that other areas show a faster rate of increase is not necessarily cause for comfort; and it should be remembered that although New York's crime rate would seem to be much higher than London's, there is evidence that, unlike London's, it is falling.

On the basis of survey data, it is clear that crime intrudes into the life of Londoners, and that for some people crime is a source of serious concern; but at the same time, there is no evidence to suggest that anxieties are markedly higher in London than in other cities.  Some survey measures suggest that Londoners are more aware of crime problems than people elsewhere, but other items show little difference.

The main conclusion that we would draw is that there is little cause to tackle London's crime problems on the basis that they are different in kind from those facing the rest of the country.  Obviously there are some features of crime in London which set it apart from other large cities - stemming largely from its role as a political, administrative, commercial and tourist capital - but London needs to address its crime problems in ways which are largely generalisable to other parts of the country.

## Crime-related issues in the London/New York survey

This paper concludes by offering some suggestions for coverage of crime-related issues in the London/New York survey.  We have not presupposed that the survey would have any explicit theoretical orientation, but have assumed that it would be aiming to provide basic descriptive information enabling straightforward comparisons.  In putting forward these suggestions, we have borne in mind that: the space for any crime component is necessarily limited; there are technical advantages to using questions that have been piloted and used in other surveys; and comparability with other surveys is a desirable bonus.

### Victimisation

The survey must clearly cover criminal victimisation, but cannot aspire to do so at the level of detail of the major national surveys.  An attractive option would be to use the battery of questions in the 1992 International Crime Survey, especially as these are being used in surveys in a number of cities in less-developed countries (for example, in Rio de Janeiro, Cairo and Manila). The questionnaire covers a check-list of 11 crimes, with limited supplementary questions (for example, on reporting to the police) for those who have been victims of crime.  Using this format would enable comparisons between a range of cities and countries.  Some thought should also be given to measuring the prevalence of sub-criminal 'incivilities' in New York and London - the extent of begging, abusive public behaviour, drunkenness and so on.

*Other crime-related questions*

It would be essential to include measures on fear of crime. Minimally, the item used in the US and British national surveys (as well as the ICS) should be used: "How safe do you feel walking alone in this area after dark?". If space allows, questions on worries about specific crimes could be included, as well as some indicator of the steps people take to avoid crime. Ratings of the police would also be essential - there are several candidate questions available. Less important, but useful, would be some measure of confidence in other parts of the criminal justice system, and some benchmark comparisons with other groups of workers. There could be interesting differences between the two cities in perceived solutions to crime, and in attitudes to punishment.

The BCS had addressed a great many other issues - for example charting the relationships between lifestyle and crimes, and examining how the social cohesiveness of areas affects crime rates. We have provisionally assumed that there would be insufficient space in the survey to address such issues.

## Notes

1. The British Crime Survey covers a large representative sample ($n = c.11,000$) of the adult population of England and Wales to assess the number of household and personal crimes experienced, whether or not reported to the police (see, for example, Hough and Mayhew 1985; Mayhew *et al* 1989). A fourth sweep of the BCS has now been mounted, and preliminary results were published in October 1992 (Mayhew and Aye Maung 1992).
2. The International Crime Survey was carried out in 1989. Roughly 2,000 people were interviewed in each of 14 countries, mainly by telephone (see van Dijk *et al* 1990). The ICS was repeated at the beginning of 1992 (van Dijk and Mayhew 1993).
3. On the basis of its postcode, ACORN assigns each home in the country to one of 11 neighbourhood groups according to the demographic, employment and housing characteristics of the immediate area.

## References

Crawford A, Jones T, Woodhouse T and Young J (1990) *The Second Islington Crime Survey*, Middlesex: Centre for Criminology, Middlesex Polytechnic.

van Dijk J and Mayhew P (1993) *Criminal Victimisation in the Industrialised World: key findings from the 1989 and 1992 International Crime Surveys*, The Hague: Ministry of Justice, Directorate of Crime Prevention.

van Dijk J, Mayhew P and Killias M (1990) *Experiences of Crime across the World: key findings from the 1989 International Crime Survey*, Daventer, Kluwer Law and Taxation.

Hough M and Mayhew P (1985) *Taking Account of Crime: findings from the second British Crime Survey*, Home Office Research Study No 85, London: HMSO.

Jones T, Maclean B and Young J (1986) *The Islington Crime Survey*, London: Gower.

London Borough of Newham (1987) *Crime in Newham: the survey*, London: London Borough of Newham.

Mayhew P and Aye Maung N (1992) *Surveying Crime: findings from the 1992 British Crime Survey*, Research Findings No 2, London: Home Office Research and Statistics Branch.

Mayhew P, Elliott D and Dowds L (1989) *The 1988 British Crime Survey* Home Office Research Study No 111, London: HMSO.

Painter K, Lea J, Woodhouse T and Young J (1989) *Hammersmith and Fulham Crime and Police Survey, 1988*, Middlesex: Centre for Criminology, Middlesex Polytechnic.

Skogan W G (1990) *The Police and the Public in England and Wales: a British Crime Survey report*, London: HMSO.

# Appendix

**Offences recorded by the police in the Metropolitan Police District, 1990**

|  | Number of offences | % of total |
| --- | --- | --- |
| **Violence against the person** | **35,521** | **4** |
| Murder/manslaughter | 185 | |
| Attempted murder | 109 | |
| Other violence/person | 35,227 | |
| **Sexual offences** | **5,368** | **1** |
| Rape | 981 | |
| Other sexual offences | 4,387 | |
| **Robbery** | **18,095** | **2** |
| **Burglary** | **174,776** | **21** |
| Residential burglary | 115,119 | |
| Non-residential burglary | 58,128 | |
| Going equipped for stealing | 1,529 | |
| **Theft and handling stolen goods** | **415,088** | **50** |
| Theft from the person | 16,000 | |
| Theft from vehicle | 135,447 | |
| Theft of vehicle | 73,936 | |
| Shoplifting | 29,652 | |
| Other theft and handling | 160,053 | |
| **Fraud and forgery** | **36,000** | **4** |
| **Criminal damage** | **144,210** | **17** |
| Arson | 5,597 | |
| Other criminal damage | 138,613 | |
| **Other notifiable offence** | **5,267** | **1** |
| Trafficking in controlled drugs | 2,304 | |
| Other offences | 2,963 | |
| **Total offences** | **834,325** | **100** |

Source: Report for the Commissioner of Police of the Metropolis, 1990 (London: Metropolitan Police, 1992).

# 4 Public space and civility in London

*Ken Young*

## Introduction: rediscovering the urban public realm

The quality of life in cities can be inferred from, or measured directly by, a wide range of indicators. Housing costs and conditions, travel to work arrangements, the availability of leisure pursuits and cultural stimulation, physical safety, are all of immediately apparent importance to Londoners' overall satisfaction or dissatisfaction with their city as a place to live. The very existence of great cities rests on a subtle calculus of personal costs and benefits, the product of which can tip abruptly in either direction. On the one hand, squalor, crowding, fatigue and, often, danger; on the other hand, the same concatenation of individuals, building and places that tires, depresses and threatens also has the power to "generate a surplus of amenity" that is the essence of urbanism (Cullen 1961: 7).

We are only now coming to recognise that people's sense of well-being in public places may be a crucial factor in sustaining or dissolving commitment to their city. The last few years has seen the stirrings of a concern with what may be termed the *urban public realm*. Less tangible, less apparent, multidimensional, harder to measure and above all more difficult to address through policy measures, the quality of the urban public realm is a confluence of architectural, urban design, transport access, policing, behavioural and cultural factors.

We do not yet know how Londoners (or indeed visitors) feel about public space. We can only guess at how far their experiences on the street, at and around the stations, in the squares, gardens and parks, contribute to the felt pleasures of metropolitan conviviality on the one hand, or to revulsion - and a resolve never to return - on the other. There is little hard evidence of the extent to which repellent sights or unpleasant encounters feed the long-term secular trend to leave London. There is a threshold at which a hitherto tolerated condition becomes a 'problem' and thus a spur to action, but we recognise it only *ex poste facto*.

Nor for that matter do we fully understand the contrary process, by which public spaces gain or regain their magnetism. We can, for example, only guess at the interplay of visual and social factors in the satisfaction of walking the recently opened-out stretches of the south bank riverside, or the nature of the conviviality that people experience in Covent Garden. The Docklands Light Railway carries large number of summer visitors through Canary Wharf, but the spirit in which they arrive is unknown to us. Responses are personal; we can see what works and what does not - for the present.

Meanwhile, there is plenty of impressionistic evidence that the negative side of life in London is becoming more immediately apparent to more people. Small incidents can send wide ripples, to be amplified and transmitted by rumour, so encouraging a process of withdrawal and avoidance: "memories of a fight in the street, or just one encounter with drunks in a town centre park" report the Comedia team, "can be enough to deter people from ever going that way again" (Landry and Worpole 1991: 16). Avoidance may well further deteriorate the quality of encounters in public places, by changing the balance of its use, thus feeding a spiral of further avoidance, decline and abandonment.[1]

However, London society is diverse, and abandonment of a place by one group may correspond to increased usage and conviviality by another. Sometimes this process of succession may establish so marked a territory that it is apt to speak of the privatisation of public space. There are underlying political issues here, of who has access to public space, and of who seeks to exclude whom. We should not be surprised, then, to find the urban public realm to be a site for contests between generations, or between minorities and majorities, be they minorities of style, ethnicity, or sexuality. The central issue is whether the resolution of conflict, where it occurs, is one which preserves public space by sustaining its shared use, or diminishes and destroys it by exclusion.

Conflicts today are closer to the surface. Every Londoner must be aware that levels of concern now run at a high level, with the *Evening Standard* in particular focusing attention on the deterioration of everyday life in London and on the decline of safety and civility in public places. The platitude that comes most readily to hand is the most-often repeated: that London is daily becoming 'more like New York'. So sweeping a judgement inevitably conflates a number of quite separate processes, as a range of quite distinct agents or processes are responsible for this decline. The broad generality of the accusation also obscures the distinction between those factors which are amenable to policy interventions, and those which are less tractable. It provides no basis for a new urban policy, while implying that new directions are urgently needed. Finally, it assumes that public social life in London is undergoing a one-dimensional, unilinear process of change.

The realities are more complex and, while we do not fully understand them, it is evident that some aspects of life among strangers in London's public places are rewarding, and possibly becoming more so, to some people, just as other aspects are deteriorating, or deteriorating for others. It is possible that steps might be taken to maintain or enhance the shared use of urban public space, leading to a process of urban revival. Recent developments in Bristol and Birmingham have been hailed as signalling "a clear shift from concern with buildings and architecture ... towards a concern with space and the quality and continuity of the 'public realm'" (Punter 1991: 24). It is more encouraging than otherwise that the degree of change in recent years has been sufficient to attract the attention of urban analysts and designers,[2] that a significant shift towards popular participation in urban design is now under way (Murray and Willie 1991), and that the once-implicit notion of the urban public realm has been rediscovered and made explicit in the debate about the future of London.[3]

It is all the more urgent, then, that the several strands of change in the complex make-up of factors that affect the quality of life in public places should be disentangled. Future policy interventions must indeed be based upon sound research; but that research must in turn be based upon clear thinking about the issue.

There is increasing recognition of the ways in which public space generally is being reconstructed by social, economic and technological processes, but awareness that places, and the functions of places, are undergoing change has little to say about *people* in places. We have charted the course of growth, change and decline in the built environment, at the expense of illuminating the ways in which people experience that environment. When account has been taken of the experience of townscape and the imagination of the symbolic structure of the city, its buildings, nodes and passages, the city in the mind has been nothing more than the physical city, subjectively experienced.[4] Until now, little attention has been paid to the most immediate and potent sense in which we experience London - through encountering others strangers in public places - and to the quality of civility in those encounters.

This, on a moment's reflection, is little short of astonishing. The classic literature of urban growth and migration, of propinquity and segregation, was a literature of people's encounters with one another; but we have lost touch with it. If we are to recognise the nature of urban conviviality and civility, and understand how they affect the quality of interactions between people in public spaces, we must reactivate a tradition that runs from Simmel and Wirth to Lyn Lofland and Richard Sennett (Simmel 1938; Wirth 1938; Lofland 1973; Sennett 1971, 1991). There has been no empirical writing in Britain within this tradition, although there is a growing richness of imaginative literature.[5] We need a fuller understanding in order to judge whether there is something here that might provide the basis for a new approach to urban renewal, one which seeks to restore and enhance the urban public realm.

**Public space and the urban public realm**

Public space is popular space, to which all have legal access.[6] It comprises:

> *the pavements and streets which become familiar as places you go in order to meet people ... public squares and malls of urban public life ... the collection of appealing buildings ... nature in the city, streams, rivers and beaches ... public transport stations and vehicles and the areas around them. Public space defines the soul and character of a city.* (Newman 1990: 273)

European ideas of civility and conviviality in public places developed in the tightly packed city, in which sociality was expressed in shared places. The ideas did not travel well, however, their export to North America and Australia showing how fragile was support for public spaces in the face of powerful impulses to extend outwards, aided by the car, in search of more generous private space.

Maintaining public space implies a perpetual search for balance in the resolution of the powerful tension between the public and the private impulses in society. The search for balance is complicated by the different choices made by different people, choices which themselves change during the life-cycle. Some people in low density outer suburbs, a study of Freemantle revealed, are happy to have plentiful private space and seek little access to anything in the urban system; others in the inner city prefer to live with little private space but appreciate easy access to public space (Newman 1990). But the maintenance of public space requires both commitment and frequent and full use.

What then of the urban public realm? We may understand the urban public realm as the social order which obtains in urban public space. It may be a social order of civility, tolerance, calm sociality and mutual enjoyment; or it may be a social order of apprehension and insecurity. Only the first can sustain the public realm over time, for the second promotes avoidance and the surrender of territory, and thus the abandonment and effective privatisation of urban public space.

The urban public realm is thus the notional correlate of physically-defined public space - streets, squares, parks, and other places where people congregate. But the two need not correspond directly, even when public spaces are planned or designated as such. A park into which we enter or a street upon which we walk at our peril is a public space still in physical terms, but it is no longer within, or is slipping from, the urban public realm.

The existence of an urban public realm is predicated on other, narrower, spheres of interaction with which it is contrasted. These are the *private realm*, characterised, writes Lyn Lofland, "by ties of intimacy among primary group members who are located within households and personal networks", and the *parochial realm*, characterised by "a sense of commonality among acquaintances and neighbours who are involved in interpersonal networks that are located within 'communities'" (Lofland 1989: 19). In contrast with these, the public realm is made up of public places or spaces "inhabited by people who are strangers to one another or who 'know' one another only in terms of occupational or other non-personal identity categories.[7]

The city is not in itself a public space; rather it contains distinct public spaces within which the private and public realms meet one another:

> *The city is not, everywhere and always, a world of strangers. The city dweller is not everywhere and always in the midst of strangers. He lives, as do all human beings, in the most emotionally-significant parts of his life, in a world of personally-known others. He does not, because he happens to reside in a city, suddenly become devoid of spouse and children, relatives and friends, neighbours and work associates, drinking buddies and casual acquaintances. In fact, his personal world may be more heavily populated than ever was that of the isolated islander, mountaineer, or villager. The personal worlds of these latter persons, however, were coextensive with their spatial worlds. When the villager left his home or the home of his relatives, friends or enemies and moved into the street, he was still surrounded by enemies, friends, and relatives. When the city dweller leaves his home or the homes of people he knows personally he is surrounded by strangers. More precisely put, **the world of strangers which is the city is located in the city's public space.** (Lofland 1973: 19, emphasis in original)*

In Lofland's analysis, urbanisation creates the problem of living among strangers, a problem for which a culture established in small places and face-to-face society has no answers and, more importantly, no ethic.[8] This might be expressed as an inversion of the question 'who is my stranger?' into 'who is not?', a question which goes to the root of interpersonal altruism in the public realm.

Modernisation and urbanisation pose a profound challenge to altruism, if only on arithmetical grounds, for as Lofland observes, interpretations of duty towards the stranger at the gate have to be transformed in an urban setting where strangers become the rule, not the exception:

> *Meeting strangers was no longer rare, it was a constant occurrence; and under these circumstances the old ways of handling them were untenable. It's one thing to kill such persons when they appear infrequently; it's another when they're continually about ... It's plausible to believe that the first stranger one sees is a god; it strains credibility to think that 10,000 gods have congregated in one place ... The old ways worked well when the small personal group confronted the infrequent stranger. They would not work at all **for the stranger in the midst of strangers.** (Lofland 1973: 12, emphasis in original)*

Hence the need to negotiate roles and rules in the city, a negotiation which occurs within public spaces.

## Public and private space in London

We have established that the urban public realm is the essence of urban life, and it is characterised by the sense of safety, stimulus, and conviviality among strangers. It is among the world of strangers that more direct and intimate contacts are made, and those who participate can withdraw for a while as they meet or make friends, business associates or lovers. In eighteenth-century London the quintessence of the urban public realm was the pleasure garden, among which Vauxhall and Ranelagh gardens were supreme. At Vauxhall

> *a concert of gay and pretty music or singing went on until after midnight, with intervals during which people took to the walks again, listened to the nightingales, paraded up and down, making friends, picking up acquaintances, or admiring the occupants of the supper boxes on the pretext of looking at the paintings behind them. Those who felt like it went into the Dark Walk, which was not illuminated, or retreated into the trees on either side of it ... The people who came were a mixture of fine ladies, clergymen, apprentices, prostitutes, dukes, officers of the guards, city merchants, pickpockets and adventurers; but the variety added to the fun, and the fashionable could always retire to the semi-privacy of a supper box.*
> (Girouard 1985: 192)

Parks and gardens were established to emulate the success of London's pleasure gardens in cities throughout Europe, most especially in Paris, Berlin and Vienna.

Meanwhile, London's prototypes fell into gradual disuse, with an emerging division in the nineteenth century between public parks as places for private display - Rotten Row, Hyde Park Corner in the 'season'[9] - and the more sustained entertainment of the music hall, itself to be repressed in turn by the puritanism of the London County Council (Waters 1989). Pleasure became a smaller-scale affair, moving from park to street, in which "the boulevardier, equally at home in London, Paris or Vienna, held court in the outdoor café and utilised the street for his amorous adventures" (Levitas 1986: 231).[10] And it moved from public to private space, today's clubs, with their discretionary membership, stratified fees and formidable bouncers, being the dismal modern equivalent of the open-air public meeting places.

Generally, so far as large-scale gatherings were concerned, eighteenth-century pleasure was displaced by nineteenth-century seriousness. Public spaces became - and remain - places for political expression, legitimate and otherwise. Trafalgar Square acquired a status as the site on which London's electoral battles, from the Boer War to the Poll Tax, were fought out.[11] Only once a year does it function as a celebratory site, and even then on an occasion of ambiguous jollity.

Since the turn of the century, Londoners have been expressing a preference for suburban and, since 1945, more distant locations, as providing more space at a lower cost, a more pleasant physical environment and a safer milieu for the bringing up of children.[12]  In large part, these moves reflected a fear of urban public life, a fear unknown to traditional ruling classes, but a distinguishing sentiment of the London middle classes.  Charles Masterman, ever the acute observer, caught it exactly:

> *The rich despise the Working People; the Middle Classes fear them ...*
> *The Middle Class elector ... has constructed in his imagination the*
> *image of Democracy - a loud-voiced, independent, arrogant figure,*
> *with a thirst for drink, and imperfect standards of decency, and a*
> *determination to be supported at someone else's expense.  Every day,*
> *swung high upon embankments or buried deep in tubes underground,*
> *he hurries through the region where the creature lives.* (Masterman
> 1909: 58-59)

London's middle class have been willing to trade off the journey to work in favour of safety and seclusion, even when that journey has become progressively longer for more of them.  Uncaring of public life, they expressed their withdrawal by migration into the significantly-entitled "semi-detached London" (Jackson 1973).  Latterly, a new equilibrium has begun to emerge as employment decentralised, opening up the prospect for millions of a more balanced and integrated - but still less urban - life in the outer metropolitan region (Buck *et al* 1986).

The residential segregation that followed from out-migration has taken a social and racial form, further accentuating the differences between the central and inner city and the safe and peaceful suburbs.  It has also found physical expression, first in the creation of tenement blocks earlier in the century, latterly in the creation of the tower block which now symbolises public low-income housing and contrasts vividly with the suburban home.  These developments, each compounding the other, sharpened the sense of difference between everyday life in the city and the suburb or country town, promoting in turn not just a lessening of commitment to London *as a city*, but a positive symbolisation of distance from London, and an exclusionary stance towards further out-migration (Young and Kramer 1978).

This process of detachment and withdrawal has been encouraged by the motor car, often identified as the principal agent in the decline of urban civility.  While there have been many attempts to define and identify the 'Good City', there is a widespread consensus that the desirable qualities of urbanity and freedom are more radically threatened by the motor car than by any other single factor.  Newman and his colleagues at Murdoch University compared 32 global cities in terms of gasoline use per capita, percentage of passenger kilometres on public transport and a number of other indicators (Newman 1990).  American and Australian cities share the characteristic of very high gasoline consumption (ranging from 74,510 MJ per capita in Houston to 27,986 in Sydney) and low percentage of public transport passenger distances (from 0.8 percent in Houston to 14.1 in New York).  London shares all the characteristics of a European city, being in the middle of the European range on both indicators, with 12,426 MJ per capita gasoline consumption, and 27.8 percent of passenger distances being covered on public transport.

The judgements derived from these figures are not however the commonly encountered judgements about pollution or transport costs. Rather, these indicators are interpreted as bearing directly upon the quality of life in public spaces: on the urban public realm. The Comedia study points up the destruction of the urban public realm by responses to the motor car: difficult pedestrian access, key sites cut off by ring roads, inadequate time for pedestrians to cross at traffic lights, menacing multi-storey car parks, rated the most threatening of urban places, especially by women, and especially at night (Landry and Warpole 1991). Yet, paradoxically, tighter restrictions on the car could further diminish urban public life in London. Pedestrianised areas, welcomed for day-time shopping, tend to be avoided at night just because the absence of passing traffic makes them more dangerous than unrestricted streets; Comedia advocate removing parking restrictions after hours, and supplementing threatened street markets with liberalised urban car boot fairs.

In a fundamental sense the flight to the suburbs, which has run at a high level for a century now, can be seen as a form of privatisation. Planners in the inter-war years readily identified this process as a flight from the public realm, one in which the gradual privatisation of domestic tasks provided much of the motive force (Young and Garside 1982).

The processes of withdrawal from public life have been accelerated by changes in technology. Of these, the partial displacement of the cinema by the home video is the most evident, although current trends are less clear-cut. The rise of electronic communications facilitates home shopping and banking. The rapid growth of home improvement centres speaks of a growing investment in DIY activities, itself significant of an inward turn in leisure activity. Far from maintaining the patterns of activity upon which urban public life can be sustained, these trends represent a deepening of the suburban impulse of semi-detachment.[13]

Meanwhile, commercially-determined trends in retailing are sustaining further changes in the nature of public spaces. First, the growth of out-of-town shopping centres and hypermarkets: these developments, as much theme parks as retail facilities, have a far greater impact in the provincial metropolis than in London. The sheer scale of London protects it from the centrifugal force that recent developments now exercise on Tyneside and in the West Midlands. The areas which stand to lose are not the central parts of London, but the peripheral suburban shopping centres in the Kent and Hertfordshire fringes.

The second major retailing transformation has even more direct bearing upon urban public space. British towns and cities are gaining indoor shopping malls, offering a standard range of shops in a fairly controlled environment. Typically these provide space for sociality; but they are privately owned and controlled by private security companies. Many are subject to electronic surveillance. They provide safe, trouble-free shopping environments for consumers, but they can effectively exclude others from access to their facilities. In short, they represent a shift from the public realm to privately controlled and ordered space. Again, these centres have a profound impact upon the small and medium-size town. Their overall impact on London is much less, but while they provide no more than an intermediate order of shopping opportunity in London's sub-centres, they represent a rather higher order of social constraint in each of the localities in which they are situated.

Trends towards the privatisation of retailing are compounded in other changes which constrain the use of the street and other public spaces. Office development and high-income housing alike show similar trends. Hugely impressive as Canary Wharf may be, the visitor's immediate sense is of security restriction; it is a sense confirmed in other, lesser developments. Luxury housing developments in London - especially in and around Docklands - typically feature high levels of security surveillance as a selling point, with the reappearance of defensive courtyard developments being especially notable. The corresponding re-ordering of land use at the micro level has had a major impact on the location and usability of public space in London. The growing segregation of retail space has created single-function urban places, crowded at peak times for their key activity, empty, alienating and potentially dangerous at others. Elsewhere, the spread of high security regimes detracts from public space less through physical exclusion than through psychological withdrawal.

Once again, the trend is to a greater polarisation. While public space persists, it becomes a space of more limited access, the values of urbanity becoming accessible only to the wealthy or - in quite other places - to the poor. Gloria Levitas captures this polarisation in her account of the decline of the street:

> *Today, the role of the street and the nature and content of social interaction vary with class, ethnic group, age structures, and type of specialisation of the neighbourhood. It is clear, however, that increasing specialisation and compartmentalisation of society **have removed indoors many of the socially cohesive activities once found in the street.** Entertainment, marketing, information, and personal services, once available on the street, are now rarely there ... In high-rise apartments, firm boundaries between the building and the street maintain separation. Only in the slum and the dwindling ethnic enclaves and blue-collar areas does the street still seem to function as a locus for public life.* (Levitas 1986: 232-3)

Meanwhile, the function of streets is itself changing. The growth of traffic and increasing mobility has the effect of opening up streets into throughways. The original function of a street, *strada* or *strasse* is:

> *an area set apart for public use and can include spaces with simple, limited demarcations without necessary connections to other streets. It does not necessarily lead anywhere in particular therefore, but may finish in a plaza or blind alley*

while the term road (and its Latin and Sanskrit roots) implies a movement to
a destination, an a-social passing-through (Rykwert 1986: 15-16). The trends
are incontestable. Yet they are only half the story of the transformation of
public urban space. Of equal importance with the re-shaping of places is the
element of civility in the interactions which occur within them.


## Urban change and civility

In order to understand how the changing patterns of human interaction
parallel changes in the spatial structure of London it is useful to return to Lyn
Lofland's distinction between private, parochial and public space (Lofland
1989). It does not correspond to the ways in which land use has been
understood in Britain, where planning has been predicated on a simple
bimodal public/private allocation of space. Yet Lofland's insight suggests that
the use people make of space may be more subtle and complex than its
allocation.[14] Moreover, a tripartite hierarchical categorisation of urban space
and territoriality has become commonplace in environmental psychology.
Lofland's treatment is paralleled in Douglas Porteous' illuminating analysis
of behaviour in personal space, in the *mesospace* of the "home base", and in
the *macrospace* of the "home range" (Douglas Porteous 1977).

Just to state these distinctions is to highlight a further possibility in the
social use of space; that part of the withdrawal has been not from the public
realm to the private, but from the public to the parochial or communal. It
would be no exaggeration to say that British planning has been pre-occupied
not with the attempt to retrieve the macrospace of the public realm, but rather
with an attempt to bolster the communal, the mesospace.

The driving force here has been the need to recreate order and mitigate
vandalism and criminality through attention to the informal controls of
popular surveillance, the watching eyes of Jane Jacobs' *Death and Life of
Great American Cities* (1972). Neighbourhoods, and most particularly public
housing estates, have been the focus of this attention. Oscar Newman's
*Defensible Space* had a major impact on thinking about communities
(Newman 1973). Neighbourhood Watch and the Home Office Safer Cities
initiative tread in Newman's footsteps. Alice Coleman has challenged the
tradition of public housing estate design, although with the principal effect of
arousing the ire of the architectural profession (Coleman 1985).

By common consent, these insights came too late to reverse the direction or
even slow the momentum of the low-income housing developments of the
1960s and 1970s, while the thoughtful Nicholas Taylor's *Village in the City*
recounts the inbuilt psychological resistance of his Labour Party colleagues
to any departure from the tower block tradition (Taylor 1973). Taylor's
contribution to rethinking London was to insist upon the provision of
*intermediate space* between the private (indoors) and the public (the external
space). The starkness of the contrast, and the abruptness of the transition, in
public housing developments precludes the manageable sociability that
Taylor's own front steps and diminutive front garden implicitly provides.[15]

British urban policy has been aimed at establishing a more congenial social order at the level of the neighbourhood. The idea of design for informal social control has permeated architectural thought, while:

> *the role of informal social control became increasingly prominent as a means of prevention [of crime] in the late 1970s. Informal surveillance - by householders, shopkeepers, bus drivers etc - was an important plank in the 'situational' approach to crime prevention developed by the Home Office.* (Hope and Hough 1988: 30)

What is controlled however is not crime, but incivilities, the unrestrained growth of which is considered to decrease the sense of communal control, leading in turn to actual criminal activity, increasing the fear of crime and encouraging withdrawal into private space, further reducing commitment to the neighbourhood, and thus leading to greater incivilities, and so on.

Incivilities are seen as a key catalyst in this spiral of decline, the appearance of 'drunks, tramps, rowdy youth, prostitutes and other disreputables' triggering increased fear, withdrawal, migration, and the weakening of informal social control that permits the growth of crime. Hope and Hough's secondary analysis of the 1984 British Crime Survey (BCS) data, using measures of victim rates, fear of crime, social cohesion, neighbourhood satisfaction and incivilities, provides fairly convincing support for this argument (Hope and Hough 1988). Types of social area are readily ranked on crime rates (burglary and attempted burglary, robbery and thefts from persons, theft of and from vehicles at home) and perceived incivilities (drunks and tramps on the streets, litter lying around, teenagers hanging around). Agricultural areas, better-off private housing and retirement areas experience the least crime and incivilities, and high status non-family areas, multi-racial areas and the poorest public housing estates the most. Victim rates appear to rise exponentially with incivility levels (supporting the spiral of decline thesis), while fear of crime has a positive, and neighbourhood satisfaction a negative, linear relationship with incivilities.

Such research teasingly raises more questions than it can answer. The incivility measures are less than persuasive, and tap only a part of the spectrum of negative encounters in public places, while the presence of litter is a weak surrogate for general neglect. Nonetheless, based as it is on a very large sample and the measurement of micro-area (enumeration district) characteristics, the potential for secondary analysis of the London responses to the BCS should be tempting.

## Encounters in public space

If the best research we have on civility in neighbourhoods is based on two weak measures of incivility, which nonetheless yield powerful findings, there is a firm base from which to move forward with research on incivility and the urban public realm. Indeed, this is the point at which to turn directly to

consider what type of questions about the experience of urban public space
in London are worth posing.

   As so often in this area, a return to basics, and to the classic literature, can
be a profitable preliminary to formulating a new research approach.
Re-reading Simmel and Wirth directs attention to three issues which are to be
found in those two classic papers, and which have been carried forward to
some extent since in research on urban public space in recent years.  They
might be termed role differentiation; impersonality; and bystander distancing.

*Role differentiation*

The notion of urban role differentiation and of its claimed "alienating" effects
we owe to Louis Wirth.  Wirth focused on the effects of scale and dislocation
on social relationships, arguing that unlike traditional, closed societies, the
social order of the city was one in which people encountered one another not
as whole persons, but as one-dimensional actors:

> *Characteristically, urbanites meet one another in highly segmented
> roles ... and their dependence upon others is confined to a highly
> fractionalised aspect of the other's round of activity.  This is
> essentially what is meant by saying that the city is characterised by
> secondary rather than primary contacts.  The contacts of the city may
> indeed be face to face, but they are nevertheless impersonal,
> superficial, transitory and segmental.* (Wirth 1938: 12)

This Wirth sees as a weakening of social cohesion and as a spur to mutual
exploitation.

   Robert Park took Wirth's insight forward in arguing that such role
differentiation established a peculiar moral order, in which individuals could
"pass easily from one moral milieu to another", in a "fascinating but
dangerous experiment of living at the same time in several different ... widely
separated worlds" (Park 1916 (1969): 126).  These Chicagoan speculations are
brought vividly to life in the London setting by Jonathan Raban's brilliant
essay on the city as "an emporium of styles", in which the psychotic East End
gangster is portrayed in just Park's terms, slipping persuasively between one
world and the next in a startling range of roles; "caught at any one moment
[Ronnie Kray's] identity had a perverse dramatic perfection" that could only
possibly be brought off in a great city:

> *the problem is that in the city - unlike a village, a club, or a Rotarian
> fraternity - appearances are easy to come by, and hard to test for
> authenticity.  For any one citizen, outside the immediate community
> of his work and family, the city is nearly all dark; moments of
> exposure are bright and fleeting ... a face here, a handshake there, a
> glimpse of the cut of a suit, the loudness of a tie, the sound of an
> accent, a quick association between the make of a car and its*

> *corresponding social type.    The city is a natural territory for a*
> *psychopath with histrionic gifts ...* (Raban 1975: 75)

- a vivid characterisation of an emblematic figure.    But do Londoners generally conduct themselves or experience others through such dramaturgies?

## Impersonality

Impersonality and its associated distancing are another recurring theme since Simmel first put forward his almost cinematic description of the city as a source of a great profusion of simultaneous and conflicting nervous stimuli; "the metropolitan type of individuality consists in the intensification of nervous stimulation which results from the swift and uninterrupted change of inner and outer stimuli" (Simmel 1938: 410).    Faced with such stress, the metropolitan man becomes intellectual in his responses, calculating in his transactions, and emotionally distant in his encounters.[16]    It is plausible enough as a description of the sensation of first arriving in a great city, but the established Londoner might find it difficult to recognise his or her experiences in these terms.    It is significant that Stanley Milgram's attempt to update Simmel's insight is prefaced with a recollection of first arrival at Grand Central Station (Milgram 1973).

  Milgram's catalogue of incivilities in public places is explicitly related to the Simmelian theory of "psychic overload", but little of it is apparent in his account of the differences in interaction styles which, he argues, distinguish one city from another.    Milgram's students placed advertisements in papers inviting people to recount incidents that seemed to them to best typify cities. New Yorkers were revealed as aloof and rude, Londoners as worldly and tolerant.    Of obvious limited value in itself, investigating this aspect of urban experience via similar vignettes could be developed in any future survey.

  Other research has in any case radically qualified the standard account of impersonality in urban public settings.    Neither Simmel's speculations nor Milgram's facile observations are borne out in subsequent studies.    Some of these are merely observational.    Wolff investigated pedestrian avoidance techniques on a crowded sidewalk and coined the term *co-ordinate* to describe the social order of the city street (Wolff 1973).    He concluded that contrary to the theory of depersonalisation:

> *it can be said that among the most outstanding characteristics of*
> *pedestrians to have emerged from this study are the amount and*
> *degree of co-operative behaviour on the streets of the city.  While at*
> *the immediate and superficial level encounters on the street are hardly*
> *noticeable and devoid of pleasantry and warmth, pedestrians do, in*
> *fact, communicate with and take into account the qualities and*
> *predicaments of others in regulating their behaviour.*  (Wolff 1973:
> 48)[17]

Again, Lofland's work has the greater penetration. She concludes with six principles by means of which people create for themselves a private symbolic shield in urban public places: they minimise expressivity and body contact, they choose their seating so as to signal no intention to interact, they minimise eye contact, and when in doubt as to what might happen next, they disattend or flee (Lofland 1973).

The important sociological point is that these devices are widely understood and reciprocated. We might ask about the frequency and extent to which Londoners find themselves employing such devices to protect themselves in public places. How consciously do they maintain distance, and in what circumstances, with what frequency, do they need to be invoked for personal protection? Do these responses differentiate conduct as between one place and another?

The aspect of London life to which these questions most obviously pertain is the sensations evoked by beggars. It is a fair assumption that the great increase in begging in public places in inner London in recent years has been registered by those who live and work there, and that different modes of dealing with beggars have been adopted. The avoidance of eye contact is a universally understood device for sustaining urban impersonality; but does its use, *in extremis*, trouble the avoider, or even lead to the deliberate avoidance of certain places? Does begging evoke compassion, embarrassment, or fear?

> *The fact that there are beggars everywhere is even more deeply disturbing. You dare not look anyone frankly in the eye for the sheer satisfaction of establishing contact with another human being, since the slightest pause will be interpreted as weakness, as warranting a plea for alms ... Here again, it is the other person's attitude which compels you to deny him those human qualities you would so much like to acknowledge in him.* (Levi-Strauss 1976: 171-172)

We might seek to discover whether this situation, described by Levi-Strauss in the extreme condition of Indian urban poverty, has any resonance in London today.

*Bystander distancing*

Of all forms of behaviour in the urban public realm none is more dramatic, nor has received more intense attention, than the phenomenon of 'bystanding'. The murder of Catherine Genovese in Queens, in 1964, in sight and hearing of at least 38 bystanders, none of whom acted even to summon the police, sparked a wave of speculation on the quality of urban life and a flurry of small, largely inconclusive, research studies.

Here Milgram is helpful in accounting for an episode of apparent massive indifference that has had many subsequent, if less shocking, replays in London and elsewhere in the intervening years:

*More than just callousness prevents bystanders from participating in altercations between people. A rule of urban life is respect for other people's emotional and social privacy, perhaps because physical privacy is so hard to achieve. And in situations where the standards are heterogeneous, it is much harder to know whether taking an active role is unwarranted meddling or an appropriate response to a critical situation ... diversity encourages people to withhold aid for fear of antagonising the participants or crossing an inappropriate and difficult-to-define line.* (Milgram 1973: 6)

Zimbardo's research, on the other hand, showed that the sense of mutual responsibility - at least towards the property of others - seemed to vary from one urban setting to another (Zimbardo 1973). Investigating the darker side of urban vandalism and theft, Zimbardo showed that these questions of altruism and assertiveness in the urban public realm go to the foundation of what Robert Park called "the moral order of the city" and pose some fundamental human dilemmas (Park 1952). These studies suggest that questions about actual experiences of bystanding, about the extent of the felt impulse to intervene in actual or hypothetical crises, about respect for the property of others and about the significance of *anticipated* incidents in the avoidance of particular urban places (or indeed the wish to leave London) would be highly appropriate instruments in any future survey.


## Conclusion: towards a new view of urban renewal

The development of ideas about the urban public realm offers the prospect of some new approaches to urban policy. Its basic contribution is to remind us that research and policy in the realm beyond that of private space has concentrated overmuch on the parochial or mesospatial domain. This is doubtless because of the focus on community and crime, and the need to create defensible space in the immediate environment of the home.

There is now recognition among opinion leaders in the relevant professions that the time has come for planning and urban design to respond to the wider questions of civility and citizenship which are implied by the urban public realm (see Tibbalds 1990). These aspirations seem high-falutin' when compared with the grimy realities of planning practice (but consider the new Centenary Square in Birmingham), yet urban public space also has a major contribution to economic revitalisation.[18]

It has for example led to recognition of what has been termed 'the evening economy', the formal and informal constellation of activities that creates life on the street at night. A strong evening economy can regenerate retail sales and in parts of London especially has a powerful attraction for tourists. Humanising urban public space with people can begin the converse spiral of attraction and reinforcement, leading to greater spending and investment and safer, as well as more prosperous areas. Again, London, with its historic areas, with its vivid ethnic enclaves, and with its street vivacity has a far greater opportunity than any provincial town or city. The publication and strong sales of ethnic guidebooks testify to the popular interest in enjoying urban public space in such places as Soho's Chinatown (McAuley 1987).

Ethnic enclaves are a happy accident in London; while they are increasingly likely to be protected and promoted for their tourist potential - as in the Bengali Spitalfields district adjacent to the expanding City of London - there is a wider cultural sharing that can be celebrated in urban public space, focusing on cultural events, but requiring co-ordination with public transport, policing, street lighting and parking policies.

We are only at the threshold of recognising the potential of urban public space to the renewal of cities. The proposition of this paper is that the quality of life and the civilities enjoyed in public places - more simply, on the street - may have a powerful effect on determining whether cities will be experienced as places of menace and threat, to be avoided, or as places of conviviality and excitement, where people will choose to live, work, and relax.

## Notes

1.  This spiral of decline argument, attributed to James Q Wilson, has been an important influence in shaping policing policy in British cities; see Hope and Hough (1988). Much of the 'fear of crime' research shows the extent to which vulnerabilities are exaggerated, and incidents inflated into trends. Research on the process of rumouring, such as that carried out by Shibutani among the Japanese community in California in the 1940s, suggests that rumour and myth flourishes in response to uncertainty as to present realities, and the approach would be worth reviving.
2.  Of particular significance is the appearance in Britain of the RUDATs (Regional Urban Design Assistance Teams) established by the American Institute of Architects; see Simpson (1991).
3.  It might be argued, for example, that threats to the urban public realm arise from excessive propinquity, leading to the growth of public legal regulation in the interests of preserving it. On this perspective, the growth of local bye-laws regulating behaviour in public places is an attempt to protect the public realm from negative intergroup encounters, in which local authorities hold the ring in the maintenance of the public realm. These thoughts were first prompted by a reading of Norbert Elias' *The Civilising Process* (1982), and I rehearsed them in "Re-reading the Municipal Progress" (Young 1985).
4.  The work of Kevin Lynch continues to be influential within the architectural tradition that dominates British urban thought (Lynch 1960).
5.  Most especially Penelope Lively's *City of the Mind* (1991) and the recently republished Patrick Hamilton trilogy, *Twenty Thousand Streets Under the Sky* (1987); see also Raban (1975), and Tindall (1991).
6.  The definitions are elaborated in Lyn Lofland's classic *A World of Strangers* (1973: 19-20).
7.  Lofland (1989: 19) quoted in Bianchini (1990). Lofland's illustration - that of the conductor/customer relationship - together with her general formulation - recalls directly the classic text of urban analysis, Wirth's *Urbanism as a Way of Life* (1938), and indicates that she writes within the fertile Chicago tradition of urban sociology.
8.  I have begun to explore the question of altruism in a secular, non-traditional society (Young 1991). The issue to be addressed in the wake of Lofland's work is the moral order of urbanism.

9. Deliciously described by Henry James in his *English Hours* (1905: 40-43).
10. The images of sexual opportunity that run through the literature on urban public space are also reflected in Lewis Mumford's fascinating 1934 essay on the photographer Alfred Stieglitz (republished as "The Metropolitan Milieu" in Mumford 1945).
11. The culmination of popular politics in public places being the London County Council election of 1907, described as the largest demonstration since the South African War, contemporary photographs showing a "very uproarious" crowd filling the Square, stretching down Pall Mall and lining the steps of the National Gallery (Young 1975: 93-4).
12. For the impact of the 1901 Census on the consciousness of suburbanisation see Young and Garside (1982).
13. Despite Alan Jackson's suggestive volume, the notion of London's suburbanisation as being a reflection of a deeper withdrawal and semi-detachment, in which the same impulses which sustained the predominant housing style of suburbia were projected into public life and international affairs, has yet to be explored (Jackson 1973). The starting point is surely George Orwell's *Coming Up For Air*.
14. This proposition has powerful support from the ethologist E T Hall in his masterly treatment of human spatial relationships and their cultural meaning (Hall 1966).
15. See especially chapter 3, "The space that lies between" (Taylor 1973).
16. The intellectual fertility of Simmel and Wirth's work is often discounted today. Perhaps this is explained by the facile manner in which some of their basic propositions have been grasped and developed, taking, for example, the density-stress relationship as a given rather than as a suggestive insight. For an example see Alexander (1973). For a critical and thorough review of a large body of recent research see Fischer (1976).
17. The same volume contains a somewhat risible account of research on the norms of subway behaviour.
18. The potential for humanising urban places through pedestrianisation is of course far from new, although a scan of European practices of some two decades ago suggests a more comprehensive and imaginative approach outside the UK; see OECD, *Streets For People* (OECD 1974).

## References

Alexander C (1973) The city as a mechanism for sustaining human contact, in Helmer J and Eddington N (eds) *Urbanman: the Psychology of Urban Survival*, New York: Free Press.

Bianchini F (1990) The crisis of urban public social life in Britain: origins of the problem and possible responses, *Planning Practice and Research* **5** (3): 4-8 (Winter 1990), Bristol: Bristol Polytechnic.

Buck N, Gordon I and Young K (1986) *The London Employment Problem*, Oxford: Oxford University Press.

Coleman A (1985) *Utopia on Trial: Vision and Reality in Planned Housing*, London: Shipman.

Cullen G (1961) *The Concise Townscape*, London: Architectural Press.

Douglas Porteous J (1977) *Environment and Behaviour: Planning and Everyday Urban Life*, Reading, Massachussetts: Addison-Wesley.

Elias N (1982) *The Civilising Process: State Formation and Civilisation*, Volume 2, Oxford: Blackwell.

Fischer C S (1976) *The Urban Experience*, New York: Harcourt Brace Jovanovich.

Girouard M (1985) *Cities and People*, London: Guild Publishing.

Hall E T (1966) *The Hidden Dimension*, Garden City, New York: Doubleday.

Hamilton P (1987) *Twenty Thousand Streets Under the Sky: London trilogy*, London: Hogarth.

Hope T and Hough M (1988) Area, crime and incivilities: a profile from the British Crime Survey, in Hope T and Shaw M (eds) *Communities and Crime Reduction*, London: HMSO.

Jackson A (1973) *Semi-detached London: Suburban Development, Life and Transport, 1900-1939*, London: Allen and Unwin.

Jacobs J (1972) *The Death and Life of Great American Cities*, Harmondsworth: Penguin.

James H (1905) *English Hours*, London: Heinemann.

Landry C and Worpole K (1991) Revitalising public life, *Landscape Design*, 16-18 (April 1991).

Levi-Strauss C (1976) *Triste Tropiques*, Harmondsworth: Penguin.

Levitas G (1986) Anthropology and sociology of streets, in Anderson S (ed) *On Streets*, Cambridge, Massachussetts: MIT Press.

Lively P (1991) *City of the Mind*, London: Andre Deutsch.

Lofland L H (1989) The morality of urban public life: the emergence and continuation of a debate, *Places* (Fall 1989).

Lofland L H (1973) *A World of Strangers: Order and Action in Urban Public Space*, New York: Basic Books.

Lynch K (1960) *The Image of the City*, Cambridge, Massachussetts: MIT Press.

Masterman C F G (1909) *The Condition of England*, London: Methuen.

McAuley I (1987) *Guide to Ethnic London*, London: Michael Haag.

Milgram S (1973) The experience of living in cities: a psychological analysis, in Helmer J and Eddington N (eds) *Urbanman: the Psychology of Urban Survival*, New York: Free Press.

Mumford L (1945) *City Development: Studies in Disintegration and Renewal*, New York: Harcourt Brace.

Murray K and Willie D (1991) Choosing the right approach, *Landscape Design*, 21-3 (May 1991).

Newman O (1973) *Defensible Space: People and Design in the Violent City*, London: Architectural Press (originally published New York: Macmillan, 1972).

Newman P (1990) The search for the good city, *Town and Country Planning*, 272-5 (October 1990).

Organisation for Economic Cooperation and Development (1974) *Streets for People*, Paris: OECD.

Park R E (1916, 1969) reprinted in Sennett R (ed) *Classic Essays on the Culture of Cities*, New York: Appleton-Century-Crofts.

Punter J (1991) Participation in the design of urban space, *Landscape Design*, 24-7 (May 1991).

Raban J (1975) *Soft City*, London: Fontana.

Rykwert J (1986) The street: the use of its history, in Anderson S (ed) *On Streets*, Cambridge, Massachussetts: MIT Press.

Sennett R (1991) *The Conscience of the Eye: the Design and Social Life of Cities*, London: Faber and Faber.

Sennett R (1971) *The Uses of Disorder: Personal Identity and City Life*, London: Allen Lane.

Simmel G (1950) The metropolis and mental life, in Wolff K H (ed) *The Sociology of Georg Simmel*, New York: Free Press.

Simpson A (1991) Planning the public realm: part 1, *Landscape Design*, 28-9 (May 1991).

Taylor N (1973) *The Village in the City*, London: Temple Smith.

Tibbalds F (1990) Private vs public realm, *Architects' Journal* (7 November 1990).

Tindall G (1991) *Countries of the Mind: the Meaning of Place to Writers*, London: Hogarth.

Waters C (1989) Progressives, puritans and the cultural politics of the the council, in Saint A (ed) *Politics and the People of London: the London County Council 1889-1965*, London: Hambledon Press.

Wirth L (1938) Urbanism as a way of life, *American Journal of Sociology*, **44** (1).

Wolff M (1973) Notes on the behaviour of pedestrians, in Birenbaum A and Sagarin E (eds) *People in Places: the Sociology of the Familiar*, London: Nelson.

Young K (1991) *Meeting the Needs of Strangers: Voluntary Action in a Changing World*, London: Gresham College.

Young K (1985) Re-reading the Municipal Progress, in Loughlin M, Gelfand M D and Young K (eds) *Half a Century of Municipal Decline*, London: Allen and Unwin.

Young K (1975) *Local Politics and the Rise of Party*, Leicester: Leicester University Press.

Young K and Garside P (1982) *Metropolitan London: Politics and Urban Change, 1831-1981*, London: Edward Arnold.

Young K and Kramer J (1978) *Strategy and Conflict in Metropolitan Housing: the GLC vs the Suburbs*, London: Heinemann.

Zimbardo P (1973) The human choice: individuation, reason and order vs deindividuation, impulse and chaos, in Helmer J and Eddington N (eds) *Urbanman: the Psychology of Urban Survival*, New York: Free Press.

# 5 Transport

*Tony Ridley*

## Introduction

Large cities seem to imply unsatisfactory transport and long and painful journeys. It is in and around large cities that the 'love affair with the automobile' of the last 40 years has come face to face with reality. It is in large cities that public transport is overcrowded or unreliable or faced with financial crisis, and public transport is frequently a place where the public is most concerned about crime.

People come together in large cities because of the rich variety of opportunities they provide. Dick Whittington is just the most famous of the hundreds of thousands who have journeyed to London to seek their fortune. People also come to the big city for culture, excitement and enlightment - to enhance their quality of life.

London provides all of this. But there are millions of Britons who heave a sigh of relief when they return to the provinces. Even when they have made money in London or found culture they are happy to return to smaller places, not necessarily rural idylls, where the quality of life is higher - at least from their viewpoint. For one thing their money goes further but above all they experience less hassle in their everyday life.

Some people try to get the best of both worlds. They live out of London beyond the Green Belt, in rural or suburban areas. Their families suffer the hassle of London only occasionally. They themselves however must travel long and increasingly difficult journeys to work every day. Above all they are not committed to London as a total place as they would be if they lived as well as worked there, shopped there and had their children educated there.

Of course London is not just one place. Bethnal Green and Kingston, Hounslow and Bromley seem to have very little in common. But London is more than one place in another sense. It is a large capital city with capital city functions - palace, parliament and government offices. It is also a large financial capital - a 'world city'. In this it competes with New York and Tokyo and, to a lesser extent, with Paris, Hong Kong, Frankfurt and probably Berlin in future.

Thus the quality of life is important for London's residents because they live there, commuters because they work there, tourists because they visit and bring lots of money albeit with attendant problems such as tourist coaches, and for inhabitants of world cities because these people are very mobile and world cities are in fierce competition with each other.

Cities are places of extremes of wealth and poverty. Historically in Britain unemployment has been seen as a problem of those provincial areas where old industries have been in decline. But the overall wealth of London, part of the prosperous South-East, has masked pockets of significant unemployment and deprivation. This has particularly been true in those parts of London which have lost their former manufacturing base.

Yet as we look ahead to the new decade, and on into the next century, we see different problems. Changing demographic patterns combined with inadequacies of education and training, could result in severe skill shortages. It is not clear whether a 'balance-sheet of skills' for the future would show a surplus or a deficit but the danger must be that it will be the latter.

This is important both to London the capital city and to London the world city. Both wealth generation and quality of life depend on good infrastructure - physical infrastructure for transport, water supply, sewerage and the rest as well as what we might call intellectual infrastructure.


## Transport

This chapter is about transport in London, its current state, its problems and the issues surrounding its future. "London Underground is a shambles", its Chairman is reported to have said recently. This contradicts the views of the Vice-President of ABB Asea Brown Boveri giving a keynote address in June 1991 to the 49th World Congress in Stockholm of the International Union of Public Transport (Svanholm 1991). He said:

> London is an example of a city that has been continuously upgrading its public transport system and has had good success.
> In Greater London, with its population of 7 million, almost 1 million persons commute daily into central London. Of these, over 60 percent use the London Underground System. Between 1982 and 1989 the introduction of a new multi-modal zonal fare and travelcard system led to massive increase in patronage, totalling more than 65 percent.
> London Underground is now modernizing their Central Line with new rolling stock and resignalling the line with automatic train

*operation in order to raise capacity. Their Jubilee Line is being expanded as the next step in an on-going upgrading. Another example is the Dockland Light Railway that is being upgraded from a one-way peak hour capacity of 1760 passengers to 8000 passengers. And several extensions of the networks are planned. Some of these will be financed either by private capital or through enhanced land values created by the railway. At the same time, the suburban network is also being upgraded. Over 2 billion pounds will be spent in the coming years on new rolling stock, stations, resignalling and electrification. A crossrail scheme is planned to link eastern and western networks with a tunnel under central London.*

*For me, London is an example of the fact that when services are attractive, enough people will travel by public transport. And as a result, 80 percent of the operating costs in London are covered by fares and other commercial sources.*

This simply indicates that everything is relative in this life. Most Londoners would express themselves as less than happy with their public transport - buses, Underground or Network SouthEast, notwithstanding the fact that ridership increased dramatically during the 1980s. New Yorkers on the other hand seem to find public transport in London a welcome improvement on their own back home.

In 1991 the Chartered Institute of Transport published a report, *London's Transport - The Way Ahead* (Chartered Institute of Transport 1991). It had the rare attribute of trying to summarise what a series of recent reports had said, to establish where there was a consensus on the key problems, to establish which solutions could be implemented without prolonged further debate and, where consensus did not exist, to see whether there was any scope for an agreed compromise.

It summed up the problems of transport in London with a quotation how it feels to be a commuter in London:

*Whereas workers elsewhere may regard commuting as a minor chore, for the London worker the journey to work is often the most unpleasant part of the day. Travelling to work in Greater London is not fun.* (Chartered Institute of Transport 1991: 2)

Commuters travelling into central London predominantly use public transport. In 1990, 84 percent travelled by British Rail (BR), London Underground (LU) or bus. However, for employed London residents travelling to all work destinations, that is not just central London, the car is the main mode of transport.

The actual pattern of transport movements in London is extremely complex. Radial traffic is that moving between central or inner London and points in outer London and beyond (that is long distance commuters using mainly BR and LU). Orbital traffic is movement between centres within the Greater

London area. This more appropriately describes the travelling pattern of London residents mainly using a car or a bus.

Although it may sometimes seem as if radial flows of traffic predominate in London, this impression is misleading as there are a significant number of orbital journeys and local traffic movements. There has been a fall of two miles per hour in road speeds in the last 10 years in the central area and current traffic speeds are only about three mph higher than they were in 1912.

With only a 6.5 percent share of the total number of commuters entering central London, buses represent a significantly under used public transport resource. Their principal problem centres on the fact that they get caught up in the delays caused by other road users, so their effectiveness is lessened by lengthened journey times and reduced reliability. Congestion and slow traffic speeds have brought about a long-term decline in commuting by bus which fell by 18 percent between 1983 and 1987.

London's buses are relatively poorly provided with priority measures. London has 40 miles of bus lanes compared to 125 in Paris. However, London's street pattern means that it will be difficult to provide adequate priority measures without disadvantaging other traffic. So, despite their obvious advantages in terms of capacity, buses are and will remain under used, unless and until they are afforded greater priority in the use of the road space.

The numbers commuting by car to central London during the morning peak have steadily declined (by 11 percent since 1983). Car, bus and coach commuters combined represent about 25 percent of the total number travelling to central London during this same period. However, it does not necessarily follow that car commuting within London has also declined.

Some reports suggest that car ownership rates and car commuting rates for London boroughs are related and forecast a 30 percent increase in the number of Londoners who would be car commuters between 1981 and 2001. There was an 8.7 percent increase in car ownership in London between 1983 and 1987, with an estimated rise of between 22 percent and 34 percent by 2001. There is pressure to increase investment in public transport to encourage car commuters to switch to rail, Underground or bus. However, there is a large and growing number of car users commuting within London for whom the car is presently the most convenient and comfortable way of travelling to work (with the exception of journeys to central London) despite the poor road network and chronic traffic congestion.

The overwhelming majority of commuters into central London travel by rail. Since 1983, there has been a substantial increase in the number of passengers entering central London during the morning peak by rail, but with a slight downturn in passengers using both LU and BR in 1990. Approximately half of these passengers arrive between 8 am and 9 am. For LU, although off-peak demand has grown 80 percent or more since 1980, the major challenge is coping with the 35 percent growth in peak traffic over this period. Sections of both BR and LU networks are operating above acceptable capacity limits.

Congestion is not confined to train overcrowding. Some 25 Underground stations suffer from serious congestion at peak periods and certain central

London stations have to be closed regularly during peak periods to avoid dangerous overcrowding. Stations at which BR's Network SouthEast services terminate on the edge of the central area are among the most congested on the network. They are also served by the most crowded Underground lines. Only temporary relief has been provided by the economic recession.

Because London is the focal point of the nation's rail and road networks, a significant volume of traffic needs to move from one side of London to the other. Taking London as a whole, through traffic covers both movements passing right through the London area, with neither origin nor destination in London, and movements passing through the central/inner London area with origin and/or destination within outer London.

It should be borne in mind that any traffic movement in London constitutes 'through traffic' in relation to some part of the area and its transport networks. On the roads this includes freight *en route* to the Channel ports. On the railways it could include, for example, travellers from Essex going into central London by train, then across London by Underground or bus for connection to Heathrow or Gatwick.

Through traffic competes for the same transport capacity as local movements and adds to the traffic-related environmental problems in the areas concerned.

At peak periods, road-based through traffic has a high level of suppressed demand. Any additional road capacity that is made available by restraint of local traffic, more efficient operation of the existing road system or new road construction, will quickly be filled unless the additional through traffic demand is to be restrained by means other than congestion.

To some extent, through movement by rail within London adds to network congestion and competes with local traffic at peak times, as in the case of roads. The actual and potential impact of through traffic by rail is, however, much less significant than that on the roads. The difficulty and inconvenience of transferring from one rail route to another (even where interchange is possible) often acts as a deterrent.

There is a marked contrast between the through movement facilities available on LU and BR systems. The Underground largely consists of lines and services passing through the central area from one side to the other. Combined with the comprehensive provision of interchange stations in the central area, this gives a wider range of through travel opportunities in those corridors served by the Underground than is possible on BR.

The advent of a Channel Tunnel terminus at Waterloo, in the absence of through Channel Tunnel trains, will have a significant impact on parts of the central area Underground system as most passengers wishing to travel beyond London will have to cross London by Underground.

Obviously the average member of the public views his transport in terms of his own direct experience. Yet transport has a much wider context. Transport must serve land-use patterns, patterns of movement of people or of goods. At the same time transport determines and develops land-use patterns. In the 1960s London was viewed concentrically, inner and outer London, with different characteristics attributed to each. Today this picture seems very outdated. Gross generalisations are dangerous but London may be better seen as two sectors of a circle.

The first, from the south round the west side and all the way to the north-east is affluent with pockets of poverty. The rest, the one-third from the north-east round to the south, is relatively poor with areas of affluence. If this is true then perhaps our transport planning ought to be directed towards encouraging development in a generally easterly direction. A start has been made with the massive redevelopment of Docklands and the extension of new transport facilities into the Royal Docks area. The intended construction of east-west Crossrail will overcome the east of London being 'cut off' from the west. The extension of the Jubilee Line through the Isle of Dogs and then to Stratford would help too.

Another major investment decision will have an important long-term impact on the shape of London, that is the link with the Channel Tunnel. Competing schemes, either direct into King's Cross or more circuitously through Stratford, will influence the way the country, indeed the world, sees the east side of London.


**History**

Any view of London today and in the future must be based on where it has come from. It is not necessary to go back to Roman times but we may note that the first stretch of what is now the London Underground was opened in 1863, the first in the world. Commuting by suburban rail services was already established by that date. The first electrified deep-level tube opened in 1890 and a considerable extension of the system took place in the first decade of the twentieth century. At that time roads were not in good repair. The roads which linked London with other cities were short of funds because the turnpike trusts which provided money for maintenance had gone bankrupt because of competition from railways. The automobile was coming on to the scene and traffic congestion in central London was such that a Royal Commission was set up in 1905. The car was replacing horse-drawn vehicles and the problem of road access from outer London to the centre was seen as a particular issue.

In 1909, Lloyd George was Chancellor of the Exchequer and he introduced vehicle and petrol tax. This potential funding led to a number of road proposals such as the North Circular and Great West Roads which were in fact built after the First World War. Inevitably their improved access attracted new development in a not well planned way. London's trains began to be electrified in 1901 and buses became part of the capital's transport provision at the same time as the arrival of the car.

In 1933, all the public transport - Underground, trains and buses though not mainline railways - came under the control of the London Passenger Transport Board and its span of control has remained effectively unchanged ever since. The trams disappeared in 1956, political control has varied between central and local government, the bus fleet has shrunk and the

Underground network has extended but London Transport provides these services today as it did 60 years ago with only the exception of what were known as London Country Buses.

After the Second World War ridership on the Underground was at a peak, 720 million passengers per year. With increase in car ownership and with decline in London's population from the 1960s there was a long and steady decline in this figure until it had reached 500 million by 1982. Bus ridership fell at an even greater rate.

Although the City Corporation appointed its first mayor in 1192, the capital did not have a directly elected government outside that area until the end of the nineteenth century when the London County Council was formed together with lower tier authorities. The area it covered however was considerably less than that of the London Passenger Transport Board.

This situation continued until 1965 when the Greater London Council (GLC) was formed; it took responsibility for London Transport from central government in 1970. At the time of its formation there already was in being the London Transportation Study (LTS) which came forward with proposals for a massive programme of urban motorway building. It caused enormous controversy and none of its recommendations were ever adopted. Construction of motorways towards but not reaching the centre did proceed, being the responsibility of the Ministry of Transport. One relic of the times was perhaps an outer 'ringway' beyond the edge of London - the M25.

It is interesting to recall what were some of the principal conclusions of the LTS and reflect whether its messages ring true more than 20 years later:

*Sweeping conclusions from Phase III of the Study are rather dangerous where there is the need for qualification on technical grounds. Nevertheless, the authors suggest the following on the basis of the assumptions made:*

1. *No road network which seems feasible either financially or politically would meet in full the potential demand for movement by road.*

2. *Whatever investment is made in the road system a substantial degree of control of movement will be advantageous.*

3. *Opportunities for the improvement of public transport by major new links exist but they are limited in number; benefits are likely to result from improvements of the existing rail system and in improving the operation of buses.*

4. *The overall use of public transport is not expected to fall, given expected levels of investment in roads and public transport; this is on the assumption that, with control of movement by road, car owners will still be prepared to make their desired trips by public transport.*

5. *Because car ownership is increasing very rapidly, even with substantial investment in roads, there will not be any increase in the freedom of an individual car owner to use his car; furthermore, if investment in roads is severely curtailed the degree of control of the*

*use of the car which would be necessary is much more severe than the public has yet contemplated and might be prepared to accept.*

*The above conclusions are based on the examination of the results of the London Transportation Study and seem reasonable regardless of the qualifications which might be placed on the numerical results. They are very much generalized and individual proposals are and will be examined on their own merits. What is much more difficult to quantify is the effect of alternative transport policies on urban development.*

*It is sometimes suggested that as London already has a substantial public transport system and that building new roads is too difficult, new investment in transport in London is not justified. Moreover London's population is falling so the money would be better spent where it is rising.*

*Surely this is a dangerous argument. People move out of big cities for many reasons. One reason is to gain freedom of easy movement. The problem for London is to improve to the utmost the accessibility of home to work, shop, school and leisure and between businesses, within financial constraints and without destroying its environment. Its future health as an economic unit and as a place which can provide for the needs of a changing population with new tastes may well depend on the provision of a modern, fast transport system vastly superior to that which exists today.* (Ridley and Tresidder 1970: 70-71)

While the LTS was being carried out the Victoria Line of the Underground was being built. It proved of enormous value to the capital. It cost a lot of money of course and one side effect was the considerable neglect of the existing system. This continued through the 1970s when, although part of the intended Fleet (now Jubilee) Line was built, the principal problem now was severe shortage of funds during a time of massive inflation.

The 1980s brought a dramatic change. A particularly left-of-centre GLC was elected with a strong commitment to public transport. Their principal policy was one of fares reduction. Legal challenge resulted in a complete see-saw. In a period of two years fares were reduced by 32 percent, doubled and then reduced again by 25 percent. However the GLC did support London Underground's proposal for a much enhanced refurbishment programme, indeed it had bi-partisan support. In addition the fares see-saw allowed London Transport's introduction of the enormously successful Travelcard.

During the 1980s the decline of London's population was halted, partly as a result of the influx of foreign professionals with the boom of London the world city's role as a financial centre, the reliability of services was improved, the refurbishment programme accelerated (though not enough to put right all the years of neglect) and the Travelcard was introduced. Ridership shot up by 60 percent in five years to 800 million.

Which of these reasons contributed to the massive increase is not clear but, undoubtedly, the Travelcard represents extremely good value for money providing, as it did, 'free' optional travel. In the early years of increase in ridership, there was plenty of spare capacity available. However, after 1986 the higher demand began to produce severe overcrowding because of the constraint of the capacity of the system.

London Underground had developed a strategy to halt decline in the early 1980s. Five years later it was time to produce a new strategy to address new circumstances. The Underground also took the initiative to work together with British Rail and the Department of Transport, culminating in the Department's Central London Rail Study from which has come east-west Crossrail, to be followed almost certainly by the Chelsea-Hackney Line.

In 1985, as a forerunner to the government's abolition of the GLC, responsibility for London Transport was transferred from it - the only example of 'nationalisation' of the Thatcher years. Separate subsidiary companies were created for London Buses, London Underground and Docklands Light Railway, of which more below. A programme of contracting-out bus services was set in motion and London Buses was itself divided into 11 operating companies. The tendering programme did not involve the bidders taking a revenue risk however and the unifying Travelcard remained in place. Thus London's buses were developed very differently to the rest of the country where deregulation was introduced.

In 1982 it seemed totally impossible that more new Underground lines would be built. Indeed refurbishment of the existing system was absolutely essential quite apart from the fact of low ridership. There was one growth area however with the creation of the London Docklands Development Corporation. It clearly needed both road and public transport investment. In a very short space of time the concept of the Docklands Light Railway (DLR) was developed and was supported by the government but only on the basis of a low, cash-limited budget for a contractor's package deal.

Then came the Canary Wharf development with the result that the DLR is now being increased in capacity, extended underground to Bank Station while extensions to Beckton and Lewisham are respectively being built and planned.

Meanwhile nothing was being done generally about London's road network. With the abolition of the GLC, government hoped to be able to resume initiatives. Four Road Assessment Studies were set up, though without any clear idea of what would be done about their results. Much of their consultation processes indicated massive concerns about public transport. Almost overnight, just before local elections, the relatively modest road proposals were scrapped.

Work on the East London River Crossing started in 1980, before the DLR had even been contemplated. Over a decade later decisions are only now being made on when the project will proceed, although its future is by no means assured. It seems that we are good at deciding not to do things, or delaying making painful decisions. But while a decision not to proceed with a project or projects is a legitimate decision, what is tragic is the failure to address the consequences of such a decision.

The failure, following the LTS in the 1960s, was a failure to face the consequences of not building new road capacity and the failure to implement major new Underground capacity, which formed part of the options of the LTS, for more than 20 years. Governments, and sadly professionals too, are well practised in explaining their reasons for particular policies and projects. We are all less good at explaining our reasons for not pursuing courses of action, and the implications and consequences involved.

## Recent times

The public is always concerned about their own individual journeys, quite understandably. Occasionally transport begins to rank high on the political agenda. This happened to some extent in the early 1980s when the new GLC made transport, or rather transport fares, a major issue. But, because it was not then an issue, congestion was not much discussed, nor was investment.

About the year 1988 this all began to change quite quickly. The King's Cross fire focused attention on the question of investment. London Underground was promoting some of its strategic ideas and the public were regularly experiencing particular problems of congestion on the M25 and air traffic capacity over London. Each of the major newspapers ran articles and editorials on the subject of transport in London.

*The Times* ran a series, "Getting London Moving", in December 1988. It made the first popular case for road pricing which many professionals were beginning to believe was an idea whose time had come - 25 years after Reuben Smeed and others at the Road Research Laboratory had first proposed it:

> *Let us suppose that from next week guests at the Ritz will no longer pay for rooms and that all costs will be paid by the government from the public purse. It is possible that this would mean there will be more guests than there are rooms. If so, then guests can sleep two, three or four to a bed. Any others can sleep on the floor or in the corridors. If this is insufficient to satisfy demand, then the taxpayer will be asked to begin providing the resources for building another hotel next door.*
>
> *This idea may, on the surface, seem impractical, but it can work - it is, after all, the way London's road system is run. In terms of land price alone, the road space in the middle of London is probably the most valuable real estate anywhere in Europe. Yet its management is curiously anarchic.* (The Times 1988)

A paper to the London Planning Advisory Committee (LPAC) was told in September 1988:

> *So far the complete seizing up of the capital's roads has only happened a few times: a manhole cover broken near Regent's Park stopped all surface traffic in north London and an accident last November at Blackfriars stopped all motorised transport as far as Hammersmith. A state visit can cause delays amounting to hundreds*

*of thousands of man-hours. Everyday we are now facing delays and inconvenience. Within five to ten years we shall be facing paralysis.*

*There is no single cause for this phenomenon. The reasons are manifold and complex: an increased and increasing population requiring a high degree of mobility; an affluent society with widening range of leisure pursuits to follow; ever-increasing car ownership; a road and street system devised generations ago and unable to cope with today's demands - never mind tomorrow's needs.*

*London once was a collection of villages with limited movement between them; today this is a homogeneous city in which work and social life require access to and from all parts of the metropolis. The demand for goods in all parts of London causes a volume of freight traffic much larger than that of 25 years ago.* (Ridley 1988: 1)

A series of reports were produced by a number of different bodies - the London and South-East Regional Planning Conference (SERPLAN 1990); the London Planning Advisory Committee (LPAC 1988); the Association of London Authorities (ALA 1989); the London Boroughs Association (ALA and LBA 1990) - as well as political bodies and professional organisations - the Institution of Civil Engineers (1989) and the Chartered Institute of Transport (1990). The Department of Transport also chipped in with *Transport in London* (Secretary of State Paul Channon) in January 1989 and *Traffic in London* (Secretary of State Cecil Parkinson) in December 1989. Note the change at the top. Political musical chairs has not been a great help to London, or to transport in London. Note too that by December 1990 we had Secretary of State Malcolm Rifkind.

In *Transport in London* the Secretary of State said:

*Our strategic framework for transport in London has five main elements:*

*Providing through-traffic with good alternative routes around London. This is why we built the M25 and why we are widening it. This is why the Dartford Bridge is being built. This is why we have commissioned consultants to see where else additional capacity is needed on routes round London.*

*Meeting the growth in demand for rail transport to, from and within central London. This is why British Rail and London Underground are undertaking major investment programmes to improve the quality of their services and to increase capacity. This is why we have commissioned the Central London Rail Study, and now the East London Rail Study.*

*Making the best possible use of existing roads throughout London. This is why the police are taking a tough line with badly parked vehicles. This is why the government is promoting new technology, such as extensive use of the SCOOT system of traffic light control and support for Autoguide. This is why the Department and the Boroughs are investing in road schemes which eliminate bottlenecks.*

*Ensuring that London is properly linked to national and international transport networks. This is why the Department is undertaking major trunk-road schemes in East London. This is why the Heathrow rail-link is to be built. This is why British Rail are investing in improvements to the rail network between London and the Channel Tunnel.*

*Tackling the congestion 'black spots' in inner and outer London. This is why we commissioned the four London Assessment Studies and the Heathrow and South West Quadrant Study (HASQUAD). This is one reason why the Department is supporting Borough schemes worth £450 million with Transport Supplementary Grant.* (Department of Transport 1989)

In 1991 the Chartered Institute of Transport report examined the issues from the point of view of five user groups - commuters, through traffic, freight, resident population and tourists (Chartered Institute of Transport 1991). The working group also went beyond the examination of various reports and made recommendations of their own.

In summary the report suggested that:

- · London's road network is inadequate but major new road building is neither feasible nor acceptable. Among suggestions put forward for freeing road space are
  - giving greater priority for buses;
  - improving the control and enforcement of on-street parking regulations;
  - introducing road pricing as a means of reducing congestion.
- Road pricing would make a significant contribution towards reducing congestion but should be seen as part of an integrated transport policy along with public transport fares, road and public transport investment and traffic management schemes.
- Very little attention has been given to the needs of the freight transport industry and to the needs of cyclists and pedestrians (the poor relations of transport).
- BR and LU systems play a vital part in moving different groups of users into and around London but congestion on the existing central rail systems has become acute in recent years and the building of new lines is urged by all. The only real issue is funding and the order of priority.

There are continuing problems created by the absence of any long-term rail development programme for London. The absence of a single London-wide focal point has resulted in a situation in which decisions of far reaching significance are being taken in isolation, on an ad hoc basis, by different authorities. Transport policies in one borough can directly affect adjacent boroughs. It is essential for transport policy to be undertaken in a coordinated framework. Most reports also agree that there should be major improvements in the strategic planning of London's transport systems.

- The UK cannot afford for London to lose its predominant position as a major trading centre. Its significant contribution towards the GDP affects the quality and standard of living for those within the south-east of England and, indirectly, those in other parts of Britain.

- There is general agreement that central government should continue to provide funds for major infrastructure improvements although there are other methods of raising extra finance.

- There is a need for improvements in the control and enforcement of on-street parking regulations.

- There is no consensus about the role of fares in covering operating expenditure but major expansion of transport networks cannot be funded entirely from fares in the long term. Opinion on the level of fares to be applied to public transport is seriously divided. (Chartered Institute of Transport 1991)

This by no means represents all the issues which are part of the current debate on transport in London but it does indicate the generality of the major questions.

## The London lobby

Obtaining political consensus in the provinces is not always easy and it is not always absent in London - witness the remarkable political consensus between the London Docklands Development Corporation, the GLC and government over the Docklands Light Railway.

Yet it does seem that people pull together better outside London. Peter Walker at the Welsh Office working with Labour authorities, the Labour-led initiative to bring Nissan to Country Durham, the total political support for the Tyne and Wear Metro, all are examples of successful regional lobby groups.

London seems incapable of this. Where is the London lobby? It does not exist (Ridley and Travers 1991). There is no all-party group of MPs which is arguing the case for the well-being of London. Even within parties, there is little effective identity of interest.

Part of the problem is sheer size. London is not only much bigger than our provincial cities, it is much bigger than Paris. It is matched only perhaps by New York and Tokyo in the developed world. A map of London Underground superimposed on Belgium would stretch from Holland, through Belgium into France.

Labour Hounslow and Islington have as little mutual interest as Conservative Bromley and Wandsworth. There have been some more hopeful signs recently. The London Boroughs Association and the Association of London Authorities are finding some common purpose on transport and the London

Planning Advisory Committee representing all Boroughs in London are doing good work, but only in an advisory capacity.

In the provinces not only do the different political parties work together, there is also a greater identity of interest between the private and public sectors. Undoubtedly the economic problems of the regions have, to some extent, forced a unity of interest and each may be acting from self-interest. But open and declared mutual self-interest can be a perfectly good basis for agreement and action.

Thus we should ask who are those who have an interest in the good functioning of London. Clearly the residents, and the local authorities represent their interest though not always to their satisfaction. But the many non-London residents who commute to London every day have an interest in London's good functioning. They obviously have a direct interest in their own commuting, but they are also interested in London's transport in general so that the services upon which they rely should operate efficiently.

The interests of the residents and non-residents alike come together in their employers. These business interests rely to an enormous extent on good access. It affects their markets and their operations and thus their bottom line.

This has always been the case but has been brought into sharper focus as London has been seen not as the national capital but increasingly as in competition as a world city. However its success or failure as a world city is crucially important to the rest of the nation.

The 'London problem' seems to be higher on the political agenda. A 'strong mayor' has been proposed and, separately, a minister for London or a new strategic authority. The Conservative Party would want to avoid apparently re-creating the GLC although Conservative thinking seems to be changing on this and many other issues. Labour, of course, might have fewer inhibitions.

It may not be too much to hope that on transport, as well as on other major matters, a strategic approach might now emerge. What is crucial however is that a consensus should be developed on appropriate policy and political and professional leadership found to push them through.

### References

Association of London Authorities/London Boroughs Association (1990) *Transport in London - Joint Statement by the ALA and LBA*, London: ALA/LBA.

Association of London Authorities (1989) *Keeping London Moving - The ALA Transport Strategy*, London: ALA.

Chartered Institute of Transport (1991) *London's Transport - The Way Ahead*, London: Chartered Institute of Transport (June 1991).

Chartered Institute of Transport (1990) *Paying for Progress - A Report on Congestion and Road Use Charges*, London: Chartered Institute of Transport (March 1990).

Department of Transport (1989) *Traffic in London*, London: Department of Transport (December 1989).

Department of Transport (1989) *Transport in London*, London: Department of Transport (January 1989).

Institution of Civil Engineers (1989) *Congestion*, London: Institution of Civil Engineers, Infrastructure Policy Group.

London Planning Advisory Committee (1988) *Policy Issues and Choices - The Future of London in the 1990s*, London: LPAC (January 1988).

Ridley T M (1988) *London's Transport - Progress or Paralysis?*, London: London Planning Advisory Committee.

Ridley T M and Travers T (1991) London Government and a Voice for Transport, *Transport Options for London*, London: Greater London Group.

Ridley T M and Tresidder J O (1970) The London Transportation Study and Beyond, *Regional Studies* **4**, Oxford: Pergamon.

SERPLAN: London and South East Regional Planning Conference (1990) *A New Strategy for the South East*, London: SERPLAN (September 1990).

Svanholm B O (1991) Public Transportation, Opportunities and Challenges in the 1990s, *UITP Congress 1991*, Stockholm.

The Times (1988) Getting London Moving, (5-9 December 1988).

# 6 Housing

*Christine M E Whitehead*

## Introduction

It is possible to address the question of how housing affects the quality of life in London in a number of different ways. In particular, on the one hand, one might take a market research oriented approach in which the emphasis is on the perceptions of those living and working in London and on the extent to which housing contributes to their satisfaction, or disaffection, with the city. On the other, one might take a more policy oriented approach, examining how those in London are actually housed and the aspects of that housing which add to or subtract from the quality of life in relation to some fairly generally accepted criteria. In this paper I have chosen to use the second approach both because this is the one for which there is a suitable range of documentary evidence and because within the UK context this is the most usual way of addressing such an issue.

In part this emphasis reflects the very different way that housing is viewed in the UK as compared to the United States (Maclennan and Williams 1990). In the UK, even under a Conservative government, housing is to a significant extent seen as a social good. In other words it is accepted that housing should be provided by the market where this results in reasonable standards at affordable prices. However it is also accepted that the government should then intervene directly or indirectly to ensure provision for those unable to find such accommodation (Whitehead 1984). This tends to concentrate discussion on socially defined criteria and the extent to which these are or are not being achieved as well as on policies necessary to alleviate problems rather than on the analysis of individual preferences. It also means that most of the emphasis is on national policies as it is national government which defines the policy framework (Department of Environment 1977). In the main these policies will not be specific to particular areas or regions but will be implemented through a wide range of local agencies - notably local authorities, whose individual powers have been much reduced over the last decade.

This emphasis also means that there is a paucity of information on individual attitudes especially at the city or regional level (see Central Statistical Office publications for an overview of what is regularly made available). Most analyses of attitudes to housing cover the whole country and are often responses to particular problems (Coles, 1991). They suggest that most people are satisfied with their housing; that an even higher proportion of households than at present both wish to and expect to become owner-occupiers; that those facing specific problems, such as at the present time mortgage possession, feel that they have had very limited housing options; and that those with housing problems look to government in one form or another to help alleviate these difficulties.

This paper therefore takes the traditional approach of providing an analysis of housing problems in London as perceived by policy commentators, together with some statistical evidence of the current situation in London as compared to the rest of the country. It then examines the way that the system operates to produce these problems, concentrating particularly on how both the role of government and the nature of these problems have changed over the last decade. Finally it identifies certain policy initiatives that have been put forward to help alleviate these problems. The paper is inherently only an overview; the bibliography includes the main sources used to build up this picture.

## Definition of the housing problem in London

The four main problem areas that are usually identified in the debate on housing in London are: first, *affordability*, both in terms of individual perceptions of their own capacity to pay for acceptable housing and the problems that arise when they cannot do so, and in terms of societal views of the maximum acceptable proportion of income that people should have to find themselves paying for housing; second, *access*, both to acceptable private sector housing in reasonable proximity to the centre and, in a mixed system of market and administrative allocation, to social housing which accounts for the majority of the available rented stock; third, *the quality of the stock*, in relation to minimum standards determined by government, with respect to both its suitability for current requirements and to aspirations, both individual and societal; fourth, the relatively low level of *investment* currently being undertaken both in terms of new building and in maintaining and improving the fabric of the existing stock.

Clearly all these four elements are very closely linked. The affordability problem relates to more basic questions about the resource costs of providing housing in London and the availability of subsidy in relation to incomes and particularly the distribution of those incomes. Inadequate access to housing is in part the limit of the affordability problem but also arises because of the mix of market and administrative allocation mechanisms and the extent of regulation in the system. The quality of the existing stock is a function of the costs involved in maintaining and improving that stock, the preparedness of both individuals and society to pay these costs and of aspirations in relation to housing quality. The level of investment similarly depends on the underlying resource costs of provision and the achievable rate of return as compared to other possible investments in both the public and private sectors.

Thus the fundamental questions are certainly seen as being economic and financial. They are to do with the resource costs of housing provision in a physically large area where there are many other potentially more profitable land uses; with the incomes and preparedness to pay of individual Londoners and particularly with relative incomes and therefore relative power to purchase the housing available; with the efficiency of both the market and the administrative systems in meeting these demands; and particularly with the effectiveness of government policy in modifying private decisions, in substituting for the market and in subsidising those unable to afford acceptable housing for themselves. They are also to do with the extent to which aspirations inherently outstrip the capacity to provide. Finally, current perceptions of housing problems are significantly about the transition from a highly regulated and administratively allocated system to one which involves significant privatisation and greater reliance on market mechanisms.

Linked to these specifically housing issues are a number of wider questions. Three such issues can be readily identified: first, the relationship between residential and employment location and the effect this has on the local and wider economy (Ermisch 1990; London Planning Advisory Committee 1991 and 1992; Confederation of British Industry 1988). This clearly links with affordability and access but it has far wider implications in terms of wage levels and the availability of suitable labour to provide necessary urban services.

A second issue is the relationship between housing and urban regeneration, both in terms of the extent to which run-down housing adversely affects an area and the preparedness of business to invest in that area and the extent to which housing investment can itself generate the climate for a wider investment programme (London Research Centre/Association of London Authorities 1987; Communities and Homes in Central London and the Council for the Protection of Rural England 1990). This clearly relates both to the problems of quality of the stock and of levels of investment but again has wider implications in terms of the necessary conditions for economic viability and growth, particularly in the inner city.

A third issue is the relationship between housing conditions and overall perceptions of the city (Royal Institution of Chartered Surveyors 1992). Housing is an important part of the environment and therefore affects general perceptions of how well the city is functioning. At the present time it is the question of street homelessness that dominates discussion but more general questions of the quality of the fabric, of access and of the extent of investment are also of relevance.

## Some background information[1]

London's housing stock consists of about 2.9 million units (Table 1) somewhat over one third of which was built before 1918, and less than 15 percent of which has been built since 1970 (as compared to 22 percent in the country as a whole (Table 2). London's housing stock accounts for about 14.5 percent of the total in England. A further 4.32 million units are to be found in the rest of the South-East (ROSE), some 22 percent of the total stock in England. London is atypical of most large cities, including in particular capital cities, in that over 60 percent of that stock is now owner-occupied (Table 1). This figure compares with 69 percent for England as a whole. Within the rented sector nearly two thirds of the stock is owned by local authorities and a further 13 percent by housing associations. The private rented sector thus accounts for only 9 percent of the total stock and less than one quarter of the rented stock. Moreover only about one half of that total is in the easy access sector. Much of the rest is let on old secure tenancies while some houses employees of the owners.

### Table 1

**Stock of dwellings by tenure**
**(000s)**

|  | OWNER-OCCUPATION % | RENTED ACCOMMODATION | | | TOTAL STOCK (000s) |
|---|---|---|---|---|---|
|  |  | Local Authority/ New Towns % | Housing Association % | Private Landlords % |  |
| **Greater London** |  |  |  |  |  |
| 1981 | 50 | 32 | 5 | 13 | 2,676 |
| 1989 | 62 | 24 | 5 | 9 | 2,889 |
| **England** |  |  |  |  |  |
| 1981 | 58 | 28 | 2 | 11 | 18,018 |
| 1989 | 69 | 20 | 3 | 8 | 19,725 |

Source:   *Housing & Construction Statistics,* Department of Environment
              *Regional Statistics,* Central Statistical Office

## Table 2

### Attributes of the housing stock 1991

| Age | Greater London % | England % |
|-----|-----------------|-----------|
| Pre - 1918 | 35.9 | 26.4 |
| 1919 - 1944 | 27.3 | 19.9 |
| 1945 - 1970 | 22.1 | 31.5 |
| 1970 + | 14.7 | 22.2 |
| | 100 | 100 |

Source: *Housing & Construction Statistics,* Department of Environment

There are estimated to be some 2.77 million households in London, some 14.7 percent of the total in England. Another 22 percent of all households live in ROSE. This suggests that in terms of the balance between households and dwellings the market is extremely tight with only about 30,000 dwelling units more than households in London and less than 150,000 more dwellings than households in the South-East as a whole. In fact the vacancy rate in London is probably six times that number, so that some households are living with others or unable to find separate accommodation. Average household size is estimated at only 2.34, well below the national average, and 30 percent of households contain only single people. Over the next ten years the number of households in London is expected to rise by about 120,000 and the number of one-person households to nearly 33 percent. As a result household size is expected to continue to fall slowly.

The numbers of new dwellings completed in 1991 was just under 14,000, some eight percent of the total completed in the country. On the other hand 20 percent of the total was located in ROSE so that new investment was undoubtedly concentrated in the South-East. Overall new building rates in the South-East are currently very similar to those at the beginning of the 1980s but are far below the historic highs of the late 1960s. Building in London itself however has fallen considerably, in part because of the very large shift away from local authority building to private sector initiatives. More than 75 percent of completions in London in 1991 were by the private sector as compared to 20 percent in 1981.

On a reasonably wide definition some 380,000, 14 percent of all London households, are regarded as unsatisfactorily housed (Table 3). These include those lacking or sharing amenities, those who are overcrowded on the accepted bedroom standard and those who live in dwellings regarded as unfit. About one third of such households are to be found in the private rented sector (almost half of those in the sector). Roughly the same number of owner-occupiers are unsatisfactorily housed but this accounts for less than ten percent of London owner-occupiers. Sharing amenity is concentrated in the furnished private rented sector as is overcrowding among small households. Lacking amenity and unfitness is concentrated in the unfurnished private rented sector, while the majority of disrepair is to be found in the owner-occupied sector.   Overcrowding especially among larger families is concentrated among those living in local authority accommodation.

### Table 3

**Households unsatisfactorily housed in London**

|                  | Number (000s) | Proportion of those in tenure |
|------------------|:-------------:|:-----------------------------:|
| Owner-occupiers  |      130      |               9               |
| Council tenants  |       99      |              13               |
| Private tenants  |      125      |              45               |
| H.A. tenants     |       27      |              19               |
| TOTAL            |      381      |             14.3              |

Source:    *London Housing Survey 1986/87,* London Research Centre (1990)

Average house prices in London are running at over £85,000 per dwelling as compared to £79,000 in the South-East as a whole and a national average of £62,000 (Table 4).   Prices have risen by about 180 percent since 1980 with a major boom in the latter part of the 1980s.   This rate of increase was somewhat greater than in ROSE and the rest of the UK.   However over the last two years house prices have actually fallen in money terms (the first time that this has occurred in Britain since the war) and are, at the best, expected to remain stagnant for some time to come.   As a result there are few transactions taking place and there are large numbers of dwellings on the market.   The recession in house prices has been concentrated in the south of England especially in London.

### Table 4

**House prices**

|       | Greater London | South-East | U.K. |
|-------|:--------------:|:----------:|:----:|
| 1980  |    £ 30,869    |  £ 29,832  | £ 23,696 |
| 1985  |    £ 44,301    |  £ 40,487  | £ 31,103 |
| 1990  |    £ 83,821    |  £ 80,525  | £ 59,785 |
| 1991  |    £ 85,742    |  £ 79,042  | £ 62,455 |

Source:    *Housing Finance,* February 1993, Council for Mortgage Lenders

Average earnings in London are also higher than in the rest of the country. As a result the average prices:earnings ratio, at 4.0, is actually lower than in ROSE and only five percent above the national average even though average house prices are nearly 50 percent higher. In terms of those who actually buy however London first-time buyers are further up the income scale than in the rest of the country. Both price:income and advance:income ratios are higher than in the country as a whole. Most importantly they have to find a 75 percent higher deposit (Table 5). Moreover these figures do not fully reflect the difficulties faced by many purchasers, especially those who bought at the height of the boom, both because the averages hide wide dispersions and because the figures do not cover those borrowing from more marginal lenders. In addition Londoners get far less for their money than elsewhere; the vast majority of those buying in central London purchase only a one- or two-bedroom flat. Even in the outer boroughs this is still the most usual purchase. In the rest of the country the most usual purchase would be a three-bedroom semi-detached or terraced house.

**Table 5**

**Dwelling prices, mortgages and incomes
(First-time buyers 1991)**

|                  | Greater London | United Kingdom |
|------------------|----------------|----------------|
| Average income   | £ 23,194       | £ 17,607       |
| Advance:income   | 2.4            | 2.2            |
| Advance:price    | 79.5           | 82.7           |
| Price:income     | 3.0            | 2.7            |
| Average deposit  | £ 14,153       | £ 8,131        |

Source:    *Housing & Construction Statistics,* Department of Environment

Rents in London have been relatively low in the regulated parts of the sector - lettings made by local authorities and housing associations and pre-1989 lettings in much of the private rented sector averaged £24 per week in the local authority sector and around £30 for housing association and unfurnished private lettings in 1989 (Table 6). These rents were only about £4 per week higher than those in the country as a whole and represented gross rates of return of perhaps 1-2 percent. Rents in the social sector have however increased quite rapidly in the last two years as a result of reductions in government subsidy and a policy aimed at bringing rents more in line with capital values. As a result local authority rents in London are now comparable to those for housing associations and are over 30 percent above the national average.

## Table 6

### Average rents
### (£ per week)

|  | Local authority | Housing Association | Private registered unfurnished |
|---|---|---|---|
| **Greater London** | | | |
| 1981 | 13.2 | 14.6 | 16.1 |
| 1989 | 24.2 | 29.2 | 30.7 |
| 1991 | 36.0 | 35.9 | 38.2 |
| **England** | | | |
| 1989 | 20.7[1] | 26.8 | 25.4[2] |
| 1991 | 27.3[1] | 32.7 | 32.0[2] |

[1] England and Wales
[2] Furnished and unfurnished

Unregulated rents which now apply to all new lettings in the private rented sector are far higher, perhaps £50 per week for a room with shared facilities in central areas and up to perhaps £300-£400 per week for a larger purpose-built flat. Even so these rents do not represent an adequate return for the landlord based on rent alone, giving a gross return of perhaps five percent on average.

Using this background information we now examine each of the main problem areas in turn, looking in particular at how changes in policy over the last few years have modified the way the system operates.

## How the housing system has operated

*Affordability*

Problems of affordability differ significantly between tenures. In the owner-occupied sector they affect new entrants who are forced to spend a large proportion of their income on housing especially in the first few years of their mortgage (Council for Mortgage Lenders, various issues). Over the last couple of years they have particularly affected those who bought at the height of the boom (especially those who bought just before August 1988 when the mortgage tax relief eligibility was changed) and found themselves with rapidly increasing interest rates (from perhaps 9.5 percent in early 1989 to 15 percent in late 1990) and often with declining asset values. These factors, together with the depth of the recession especially concentrated in the services sectors and in the south, have hit Londoners worse than elsewhere resulting in large increases in mortgage arrears and a growing number of repossessions.

In the social sector problems of affordability arise mainly from increases in rents as a result of changes in government policy and from the form of the housing benefit system. On the one hand central government has required local authorities to raise rents (by reducing subsidy) and has similarly forced housing associations to cover a larger proportion of their costs from rents. These policies have only just started to bite but it is expected that rents in all parts of the social sector will rise in real terms over the next few years. Households on very low incomes are fully protected from these rises by the form of the housing benefit system which pays 100 percent of rents for those with incomes below a certain income level (based on household needs) and pays all increases in rents for all those in receipt of any housing benefit. However this subsidy is withdrawn rapidly above these income levels so that 65 percent of every additional £1 of income is lost as a result of benefit withdrawal. Almost everyone (except those living in the highest rented properties) who is in full-time work is thus ineligible for assistance. Low-income employees can therefore find themselves paying significant proportions of income in rent even though these rents are themselves very low by market standards. Over two thirds of tenants in the social sector are eligible for benefit but there is a real problem of affordability, especially by historic standards for many of the other tenants (London Planning Advisory Committee 1988; Hills 1991).

In the private rented sector the problem is fairly clearcut. Many of those seeking accommodation are lower-income households, while there is a shortage of adequate accommodation at reasonable rents (Whitehead and Kleinman 1987; London Research Centre 1991). The typical result is that single people group together and pay high rents in relation to income for poor quality accommodation, especially as compared to the major tenures. Tenants on the lowest incomes are eligible for benefit as in the social sector while many of those who have lived in their accommodation for some time have secure tenancies. The problem is therefore concentrated among new entrants and those with incomes somewhat above the minimum.

*Access*

Access problems similarly vary between tenures. Clearly access to owner-occupation depends upon capacity to pay. Deregulation of the finance market has meant that in the 1980s it has been possible for households to borrow a far larger multiple of household income than in the past as well as a higher proportion of the purchase price. Indeed some have borrowed significantly more than 100 percent of the assessed value of the property. This has increased access to owner-occupation but also increased problems of affordability.

Government has concentrated much of their housing policy in the 1980s on privatisation including not only the right to buy but also shared ownership schemes and other low-cost home ownership initiatives. These have helped to make owner-occupation available to more than 60 percent of London households even if some of these households have found it difficult to pay. It has also reduced ease of access to social housing.

At the present time most of the emphasis in the owner-occupied market is on the effect of the recession and particularly the growing problems of arrears and repossessions on the overall operation of the owner-occupied market. The number of transactions has fallen significantly making it difficult for people to adjust their housing circumstances either in relation to job change or other reasons for moving or to sell their dwelling if they get into financial difficulties. Moreover the large numbers of dwellings that have been repossessed overhang the market reducing confidence in its revival and further slowing down sales. These conditions have brought housing into the centre of political debate. The problems are probably worst in London because the boom was also greatest there and because of the large numbers of first-time buyers who entered the market in the late 1980s (Council for Mortgage Lenders, quarterly reviews).

The major problems of access however still relate to those households unable to afford owner-occupation (Bramley 1990, 1991; Kleinman and Whitehead 1991). Access to the social rented sector has become much more difficult over the last decade both as a result of the loss of dwellings through the right to buy and other transfer policies and because of the cutbacks in the new building programme. Of the 57,000 local authority lettings available in London in 1989, 28 percent went to statutorily homeless families and only 11 percent went to households on the normal waiting list (Table 7). Thus only about 6,000 Londoners without priority need were housed in the local authority sector that year. The number of lettings made by housing associations has similarly fallen as a result of cutbacks in their investment programme. These are now being reversed but at the same time associations are being required to concentrate their programmes more on housing the homeless, so access for traditional types of household is being further restricted.

Table 7

Local authority lettings
(1989 - 1990)

|  | Homeless | Key workers | Waiting list | Non-secure tenancies | Transfers | Total (000s) |
|---|---|---|---|---|---|---|
| Greater London % | 28 | 5 | 11 | 17 | 39 | 57,000 |
| England % | 17 | 4 | 32 | 5 | 41 | 390,000 |

Source: *Regional Trends No 26*, Central Statistical Office

For those households unable to obtain access to either owner-occupation or social rented housing the only options are to leave London or to find accommodation in the private rented sector (Whitehead and Kleinman 1987). The history of regulation of both rents and security of tenure with respect to dwellings where the landlord is not resident, together with a tax system which favours owner-occupation has led to a precipitous decline in the availability of private lettings throughout the post-war period.    The government deregulated private lettings in the 1988 Housing Act, introducing assured tenancies where rents could be set at market levels but tenants had security of tenure or assured shorthold tenancies, where there is only contractual security.    They also introduced a limited scheme of providing large tax benefits to new landlords under the Business Expansion Scheme (BES) (Crook *et al* 1991).    These measures, together with the recession in the housing market, have probably increased the numbers of new lettings available in London.    However the traditional, regulated part of the sector continues to decline and there is no certainty that political risks and/or the revival of the owner-occupied market will not reverse this increase.    The private rented sector therefore remains extremely restricted in comparison to almost any other major city.    As a result new and indeed mobile households are often forced to buy while those on lower incomes obtain poor quality lettings and poorer value for money.

At the limit there are growing problems of homelessness and rooflessness (Audit Commission 1989; Greve 1990).    Local authorities are required to house families that are statutorily homeless.    These include families with children or individuals at risk because of age or sickness who are accepted as in need of accommodation and who are 'involuntarily' homeless.    Authorities are not required to house other single people or married couples without children.    In 1989 some 34,000 households were accepted as statutorily homeless in London.    This accounted for over one quarter of all such acceptances and represents a rate per head of population almost twice that in the country as a whole.    Many of these were housed either in non-secure tenancies (short-life properties or in units leased from the private sector) or in bed and breakfast accommodation.    Government has introduced a range of policies to improve the flow of more suitable short-term accommodation. These have had some success.    However the numbers of households presenting themselves as homeless have continued to increase and there are major problems with respect to the availability of longer-term secure accommodation.

Those unable to find their own accommodation who are not statutorily homeless may ultimately find themselves on the street.    The problems of street homelessness were almost unknown at the beginning of the 1980s but grew rapidly during the decade especially in central London.    There are thought to be three main reasons: the closure of long-stay mental institutions and large-scale hostels for the homeless, cutbacks in social security for younger people which mean that those who leave home (or more usually children's homes) without a job find it difficult to find secure accommodation, and simply the tightness of the London housing market. Estimates of the numbers of such street homeless vary considerably from as low as 1,000 to over 5,000.    The government has pledged that they will ensure that there are adequate numbers of hostel beds available.    As a result the problem has declined somewhat in 1991 but many still remain on the street while others are accommodated on a night to night basis.

It has been estimated that there may be nearly 400,000 households in need of acceptable rented housing in the capital if account is taken not only of the homeless and inadequately housed but also of potential households living with other people (London Research Centre 1990b). At the present time the only chance of additional provision is either through housing associations, whose programmes are constrained by the availability of subsidy, or through the private rented sector which could utilise existing units more effectively. The other possibility is that falling house prices will ease access problems to the owner-occupied sector. However if more households were able to afford such housing it can be assumed that prices would soon rise again as there is very little prospect of large-scale additional provision. Most commentators therefore do not expect to see much significant improvement in terms of access for lower-income households over the next few years.

*The quality of the stock*

London's housing stock is relatively old. Moreover there were large-scale slum clearance programmes in the 1950s and 1960s in which Victorian privately rented housing was replaced both by high-rise local authority housing and by a programme of population dispersal to new towns and outer estates. As a result much of the inner area local authority stock, while relatively new, is regarded as undesirable. This causes major problems of estate management and the need for refurbishment and at the limit demolition. Local authorities have been able to increase their investment in the existing stock over the last decade using some of the realised assets from the right to buy programme. Government has also introduced a wide range of specific policies such as Estate Action and City Grant which emphasise both physical improvement and tenure diversification. They also see large-scale voluntary transfers and Housing Action Trusts as ways of introducing new funding and better management. However by no means all the problems on these estates arise from their physical attributes. In particular, a large proportion of tenants are non-participants in the labour force, incomes are low and morale is often lower. High turnover rates also mean that the highest priority tenants get concentrated in these 'sink' estates.

In the private sector the problem is more one of disrepair. Grant aided improvements have reduced the number of dwellings without amenities very considerably (Department of Environment 1988). However the number of dwellings in need of over £7,000 worth of repairs is believed to have grown throughout the decade. In part this reflects a difference between individual wishes and accepted standards, especially among the old who may not want the disruption of doing significant repair work; in part it reflects cash flow problems. However, in the main it reflects the low incomes of many owner-occupiers especially among the elderly and the low rates of return available to private landlords, where many of the worst problems of disrepair are concentrated.

Housing associations have played a special part in the rehabilitation of the existing stock especially in inner London. In some areas they have been the main source of investment in neighbourhood upgrading. The cutbacks in housing association subsidy in the 1980s, together with the change in subsidy framework by which associations now bear the risk of cost overruns have reduced this role, leading to considerable worries about how neighbourhood regeneration is to be organised in the future.

*Investment*

We have already noted how the number of completions has fallen in London over the last decade. The main reason for this decline has been the very rapid reduction in the local authority building programme which has been reduced from over 13,000 units in 1981, and higher levels in the 1960s and 1970s, to fewer than 1,000 in 1989 (Brownhill *et al* 1990; Kleinman 1991). Moreover it is this government's intention that local authorities should no longer play a role in the direct provision of new accommodation, except for certain types of special needs, but instead should act as enablers to other providers, notably housing associations. This role includes making land available at subsidised prices as well as other forms of partnership.

The level of housing association investment depends crucially on the amount of grant that the government is prepared to make available (National Federation of Housing Associations 1992). Associations receive capital grants covering an average of 70-75 percent of the costs of provision. In London these proportions are higher, especially for rehabilitation schemes. The rest of the finance must be procured from the private sector at market rates of interest. Associations then bear the risk of development or purchase and set rents to cover costs, perhaps with some cross-subsidy from existing schemes. London associations are finding it extremely difficult to operate within the cost limits and still be able to let at affordable rents. Moreover these costs limits have been much reduced because government argues that the recession allows far better bargains to be struck. Associations are finding it even more difficult to accept the risks involved in rehabilitation schemes so the emphasis has moved away from both development and rehabilitation to buying 'off the shelf' from the private sector. Finally, associations have been asked to include shared-ownership projects in their programmes but have found the risks involved even greater than for other types of development. As a result government is moving to DIY shared ownership which will involve purchasing property from the private sector rather than additional investment. Despite these problems housing association investment in London will undoubtedly increase over the next few years. However it is unlikely to expand enough to offset the cutbacks in local authority provision.

In the private sector there is little evidence to suggest that private landlords find new investment worthwhile except to a very limited extent with respect to BES schemes. The vast majority of new building is therefore for the owner-occupied market. Here the main problem at the present time is lack of demand because of the overhang from the boom in 1988-89. Even now there are large numbers of unsold newly-built dwellings especially in and around Docklands.

In the longer term the problem is more one of supply constraints and particularly of land availability (London and South-East Regional Planning Conference 1990). During the 1980s housing land prices increased by nearly 800 percent as demand from developers expanded rapidly (Table 8). As a result land costs accounted for more than 60 percent of the cost of new building in 1989. Since then land prices have fallen back mainly as a result of declining expectations about dwelling prices. However there is little doubt that when demand does pick up land prices will again rise unless something is done to change the availability of land for housing production. As a result of these land availability problems it is suggested by government that many of the 200,000 units which their Strategic Guidance states should be provided in London over the next decade should come from existing units or from buildings transferred from other uses. Private builders on the other hand would like to build mainly on green-field or infill sites. This raises extremely difficult land use planning problems, especially if the current extensive green belt policy is to be maintained. In current economic conditions however the problem remains one of demand, both private and public. As a result it seems highly unlikely that new provision in London will achieve anything like the projected number of units before the end of the century.

Table 8

**Housing and land prices**

|  | Greater London | England |
|---|---|---|
| **Housing land price per hectare** | | |
| 1981 | £   391,000 | £ 111,800 |
| 1989 | £ 3,090,900 | £ 451,600 |
| % increase | 790 | 404 |
| **Average new dwelling price** | | |
| 1981 | £ 35,800 | £ 28,500 |
| 1989 | £ 85,200 | £ 78,300 |
| % increase | 238 | 275 |
| **Land as proportion of dwelling price** | % | % |
| 1981 | 27 | 63 |
| 1989 | 16 | 25 |

Source: *Regional Trends No 26*, Central Statistical Office

We have already discussed the question of investment in the existing stock under quality. Levels of investment by the social sector depend on both the form and availability of subsidy. Local authorities have increased their improvement programmes over the decade but, given the nature of their stock and their financial constraints, are unable to tackle many of the worst problems. The government's policy of transferring these estates to other landlords in order, in part, to increase the pace of change is only in its infancy. The financial regime in which housing associations operate has, if anything, reduced their immediate capacity to undertake improvements. On the other hand they are now required to make provision for major repairs in the future. The general impression, unconfirmed as yet by statistics, is that the backlog of necessary investment is increasing.

In the private sector improvement investment is determined more by market factors. Changes in the improvement grant system, making eligibility income rather than dwelling related, is expected to result in less investment being undertaken. But the more basic questions are those of income and capacity to pay, available cash flow and most simply whether private owners wish to achieve the sorts of quality that society regards as satisfactory. Thus the problem comes full circle to one of aspiration and affordability.


## Key questions

### The roles of central and local government

Perhaps the most obvious factor that emerges from this description is the importance of central government policy in determining the current situation. It is central government in particular that specifies both the levels of financial assistance to local authorities and the allocation of that funding to particular areas. Local government's role is limited to the management of its own stock, its enabling role in relation to other providers and to carrying out its statutory functions with respect to land use planning, monitoring standards and housing the homeless. This is clearly a very different position from the traditional role of authorities which included the power to determine their own investment programmes within unit cost limits and to cross-subsidise both between dwellings and between ratepayers and tenants.

The main difference between London and the rest of the country in terms of that subsidy system has been the extent to which it has recognised that costs are higher than elsewhere and therefore that larger subsidies are necessary to ensure affordability. To some extent government is changing this situation and reducing that subsidy by increasing rents in line with capital values and giving incentives to develop in cheaper areas.

London also differs from much of the rest of the country in the extent to which it attracts people from other parts of the country and abroad because of better employment possibilities, the range of services available and simply the nature of a capital city. Yet it is extremely costly to provide adequate housing within the capital itself and this causes tensions both because those who have lived in London all their lives (and especially the children of such households) may be forced further out by the market, and because policy on the whole attempts to solve problems where they arise.

The traditional way of addressing these problems has been through local authority intervention (Whitehead and Cross 1991). In London prior to 1965 the London County Council (LCC) played a strategic role in the provision of affordable housing itself producing over 200,000 units, organising a large-scale slum clearance and replacement programme, maintaining the green belt and implementing a overspill policy by which large numbers of Londoners were rehoused in new and expanding towns. When the Greater London Council (GLC) replaced the LCC it maintained the strategic planning role and continued to add to its stock. At the same time the London boroughs continued to increase their provision. However after 1979 the GLC was required to transfer its stock to the boroughs. On the abolition of the GLC what strategic role remained was taken over by the Secretary of State for the Environment. The Secretary of State issues planning guidance which specifies the need for new housing provision over the next decade by all sectors on the advice of the London Planning Advisory Committee. No other strategic housing role remains.

The powers of the local authorities have similarly been eroded. Authorities can invest very little without central government permission and will not generally receive permission to add to their stock. They may not subsidise their tenants from local taxes. They must allow tenants who wish to buy their own property to do so and at the limit must transfer their stock to another landlord if the tenants so desire. They keep the responsibility for housing homeless households and are expected to play an enabling role in helping other providers, mainly housing associations, to increase the supply of affordable housing. Their two main powers here are the capacity to transfer land owned by the authority to such providers at below market prices and their planning role, by which they can attempt to make more land available for housing, to assist change of use to housing or to negotiate planning gain agreements which include some affordable housing provision in large-scale mixed developments.

Thus one key issue in the provision of adequate housing in London is the lack of any strategic housing authority and the transformation of the role of local government from the main provider of rented housing to lower-income households to one in which at the most it simply maintains its existing stock and helps others to meet current needs. Thus the role of central government which controls the finance available to these other providers has become far more dominant.

*Housing associations and other social providers*

A second key issue is the capacity of housing associations and other social landlords to fill the gap left by the withdrawal of local authorities (National Federation of Housing Associations 1992).

During the 1980s central government cutbacks in finance reduced housing association investment programmes.  At the same time their form of subsidy was changed so that instead of acting within an extremely tight regulatory framework associations were forced to take some of the risks and were also given powers to set their own rents.  They were also required for the first time to raise their additional financing requirements from the private market.  Within this context they are being asked to increase their levels of investment (however often by buying off the shelf from private developers rather than through their own development or through rehabilitation), to ensure that a large proportion of their lettings go to homeless families (most association properties are filled by tenants nominated by local authorities), to be involved in a range of special government initiatives especially with respect to shared ownership schemes and short-term leasing schemes for the homeless and roofless, and in some cases to take over the management of local authority housing.  Moreover given the current levels of subsidy and of cost indicators many associations are no longer certain that they can continue to operate in such a way that rents can remain affordable for those just above benefit levels.  The complexity of their operations has therefore increased manyfold in the last few years.

The immediate constraint on association activity is undoubtedly the level of government subsidy available to associations through the Housing Corporation.  London receives a more than proportionate share of these national funds, reflecting both the higher costs and the extent of access problems in London.  Moreover, these funds are expected to increase rapidly over the next few years.  Even so, associations argue that they are being heavily constrained and in particular that subsidy rates are inadequate given the incomes of their tenants and the costs of operating in the capital.  A rather different question is whether, if another government were to be prepared to increase this funding even more rapidly associations would be effectively placed to use these funds efficiently to increase the supply of affordable rented housing in London.

The London Dockland Development Corporation also has the potential to play an important role in increasing provision.  Development plans for the area include large quantities of housing together with a commitment that 40 percent of this housing will be affordable and available to local households.  In practice these plans have currently come to a halt, both because of the recession in the housing market (there are said to be over 30,000 unsold units in Docklands at the present time) and because other types of development have also come to a halt so that there is no current potential for cross-subsidy.  However in the longer term, and especially if transport links improve, Docklands and the surrounding areas may provide a significant opportunity to increase the stock of housing close to employment within the central area for households of every income group.

## The private rented sector

The most obvious problem in London in comparison to other major cities is the small size of the private rented sector and the even smaller element of that sector which is readily available to new and mobile households (London Planning Advisory Committee 1991, 1992). This situation has arisen not only from the stringent rent controls and security provisions which existed from before the Second World War until 1988, but also because the tax system has favoured owner-occupation reducing the incentive either to demand or to supply rented accommodation.

The government deregulated the private rented sector in 1988 allowing all lettings to be at market rents with varying extents of security. However many problems remain before we can expect to observe a viable large-scale easy access sector (Best *et al* 1992).

First, there are continuing problems of political risk - will a different government re-introduce controls? This cannot be answered until a change of government has been observed. This must be some time ahead; moreover the Labour Party's position has moved strongly towards deregulation over the last couple of years. Second, there is simply a problem of demand. Even in current circumstances the majority of potential private tenants have very low incomes and therefore very little capacity to pay the rents necessary to provide an acceptable rate of return. Housing benefit is available to cover these rents but there are significant transaction costs and uncertainties surrounding the process, so that many potential landlords do not think that letting is worthwhile. Third, there is simply a lack of expertise and experience not only among potential larger landlords but also in the private finance market which would have to provide the finance for expansion. It will, at the best, take a long time to produce a viable private market able to offer choice to those further down the income scale.

## Land availability

Prices in the private sector depend upon supply and demand. The demand for owner-occupation has been high and increasing until the last couple of years and as a result house prices have risen in real terms very considerably. The outcome of this process has not in the main been additional investment especially in new building but rather higher land prices. Unless more land can be made available this situation will simply be repeated when demand again increases.

The land use planning system provides very strict constraints on the transfer of land between uses and the type of development that can be undertaken (Department of Environment 1992a). Local authorities around London face strong pressures to limit development in order to preserve the nature of their communities. Although they are required to ensure that adequate land is made available for necessary expansion they also have some control over the estimates of what is required. Moreover, they can attempt to locate development land in areas which will cause them the least difficulty in local political terms. In current circumstances much of the emphasis is placed on the reuse of land and buildings and to a lesser extent on infill development. All these options are relatively expensive. So far the green belt has been regarded as sacrosanct which implies that if large-scale additional investment is to be made available it will have to take place outside the Greater London area. Authorities in these areas have little or no incentive to accept such development.

There are two areas where additional large-scale provision is seen a potentially acceptable - the redevelopment of Docklands and the development of the east Thames corridor. The second would involve modifying the green belt which is likely to be politically extremely difficult. It also involves, as does Docklands, immense investment in infrastructure. Both such developments will take a long while to make any significant impact on London's housing problems, and are unlikely to occur.

*Access and capacity to pay*

Underlying all these problems are the two most basic questions: whether Londoners can afford to pay for adequate housing given real resource costs, the extent of central government subsidy and the underlying distribution of income, and whether the housing system is adequately flexible to respond to all types of demand. Land in London has many uses and housing is not necessarily the most profitable. Housing is always therefore going to be relatively expensive - even if planning constraints are reduced. Those on higher incomes will necessarily bid up the prices of what housing is available, forcing lower-income households to move to less desirable areas, to pay higher proportions of their income for housing and to consume less in terms of both quality and quantity. In the past this process has been offset by the large-scale provision of social housing at heavily subsidised rents. By increasing rents, limiting local government involvement and shifting at least some of the subsidy from supply to the individual the government has transferred some of these problems into the market sector. Housing benefit at least in principle completely protects those on the lowest incomes but leaves a major problem of capacity to pay among those slightly further up the market.

Government schemes to assist lower-income households into home ownership and shared ownership alleviate some of these difficulties. But home-ownership is not suitable for many lower-income households. There therefore remains a large gap between those who can afford owner-occupation and those who have gained access to social housing which at the present time can only be filled by the private rented sector or by housing associations. The existence of housing benefit for market rents should imply that the market will meet all types of demand at a price. However, the evidence so far is that this is not the case. At the limit people are unable to find any accommodation they can afford and become homeless and roofless as a result of both lack of income and limited access to either social housing or private renting. The problem then becomes one of whether the government is prepared to pay to solve these problems specifically in London through additional subsidy and investment.

## Current policy initiatives

Not surprisingly in this context most of the suggested policy initiatives concentrate on increasing government subsidy to social housing providers. They include increasing the allocation of Housing Association Grant to London housing associations, both by increasing the total and by reallocating in relation to the incidence of homelessness; giving local authorities permission to spend all the receipts that they have received from the right to buy and the sale of land; and, more generally, allowing local authorities to maintain and expand their housing role rather than to reduce their involvement as is currently envisaged.

The second major constraint is seen to be in terms of land availability and the operation of the planning system (Department of Environment 1991b, 1992a). The most radical approach here would entail breaking the stringent controls which limit development in the green belt and allowing development in certain specified areas notably in the eastern corridor. This would link up with other policies to reduce congestion and improve the transport system and with existing policies such as those which include large-scale housing developments in the Docklands project by means of 'compacts' with the local authorities to provide affordable housing both for rent and shared ownership. There is also considerable pressure to ensure that all housing developments include a proportion of affordable housing, a policy first introduced in parts of the United States. In the inner city the problem, and solution, is more likely to be one of encouraging change of use (Brownhill *et al* 1990).

Probably the most important immediate policies involve improving the management of and access to the existing stock, especially to the private rented sector. Here the most successful approach appears to be the extension of private leasing schemes by which housing associations manage property owned by private landlords to provide short-term accommodation for homeless households (London Research Centre 1990b). Extensions could include lengthening the maximum lease and providing incentives on both sides to enter into long-term management arrangements. DIY shared ownership by which social sector tenants are given subsidies to find their own private housing and thus release rented property for needier households are also likely to grow in importance.

Finally there is a growing emphasis on improving the management of local authority housing by requiring compulsory competitive tendering for all management services, by extending the estates action and priority estates programmes which concentrate on improving the quality of life on the worst local authority estates and by transferring management to Housing Action Trusts (Audit Commission 1992; Department of Environment 1992b).

The most obvious attribute of these policy proposals is that almost all of them depend upon changes in central government policy. Local authorities have little independent authority while London Planning Advisory Committee acts only in an advisory capacity to the Secretary of State on planning issues.

The second obvious aspect is that the policies almost all relate to economic or financial instruments. There is little debate about housing at the environmental or the aesthetic level, except with respect to maintaining the fabric of the existing stock and controlling the spread of street homelessness (Royal Institution of Chartered Surveyors 1992).

The third point is that there is little discussion about the situation faced by those in the owner-occupied market except with respect to current problems of arrears and repossessions. Owner-occupation is still regarded as a desirable policy aim and is still desired by the vast majority of Londoners. On the other hand while there is continuing discussion about the importance of a healthy private rented sector there are few policy initiatives directed at improving supply. The combination of deregulation and the availability of housing benefit (together with the current difficulties in the owner-occupied sector) are seen by government as providing an adequate basis for revival. Rents have certainly fallen and availability of short lets increased. On the other hand homelessness acceptances continue to increase.

In the UK context policy initiatives have little chance of success unless they are accepted by central government. The very large changes that the Conservative government has introduced over the last decade and more have shifted the emphasis away from social provision towards an enabling role for local authorities and a wider range of landlords (Audit Commission 1992). They have also significantly increased the direct cost of housing to most households. These policies have helped exacerbate the problems of affordability and access for lower-income households especially in London and the South-East while increasing choice for many households further up the income scale.

Overall the vast majority of Londoners remain satisfied with their housing and are housed in reasonable quality accommodation at prices that are within their means. The problems discussed above affect only a small proportion of Londoners and are in the main not specific to London. Nor are environmental problems seen as being particularly housing specific, except with respect to local authority estates and street homelessness. Housing is certainly of basic importance for the quality of life in London and house prices and rents are major factors determining the standard of living achieved by London households. Housing is also an important national policy issue in terms of the operation of the economy as well as of housing conditions. Yet in terms of this discussion housing is clearly nowhere near as central to people's evaluation of London as either education or transport.

**Note**

1.  This section gives only a limited overview of the position. For a more detailed analysis see Whitehead and Cross 1991.

# References

Audit Commission (1992) *Developing Local Authority Housing Strategies*, London: HMSO.

Audit Commission (1989) *Housing the Homeless: The Local Authority Role*, London: HMSO.

Best R, Kemp P, Coleman D, Merrett S and Crook A (1992) *The Future of Private Renting*, York: Joseph Rowntree Foundation.

Bramley G (1991) *Bridging the Affordability Gap in 1990*, Bristol: SAUS.

Bramley G (1990) *Bridging the Affordability Gap*, Bristol: SAUS.

Brownhill S, Sharp C, Jones C and Merrett S (1990) *Housing London*, York: Joseph Rowntree Foundation.

Central Statistical Office (annual) *Social Trends*, London: HMSO.

Central Statistical Office (annual) *Regional Trends*, London: HMSO.

Central Statistical Office (1991) *General Household Survey 1989*, London: HMSO.

Communities and Homes in Central London and the Council of Protection of Rural England (1990), *Home Truths*, London: CHiCL/CPRE.

Coles A (1991) Changing Attitudes to Owner-Occupation, *Housing Finance*, **11**, London: Council of Mortgage Lenders.

Confederation of British Industry (1988) *Special Survey of Company Housing Needs in the South-East*, London: CBI.

Crook A, Kemp P, Anderson I and Bowman S (1991) *The Business Expansion Scheme and Rented Housing*, York: Joseph Rowntree Foundation.

Council for Mortgage Lenders (1991) *Housing Finance*, London: Council for Mortgage Lenders (August 1991).

Department of Environment (quarterly and annual) *Housing and Construction Statistics*, London: HMSO.

Department of Environment (1992a) *Planning Policy Guidance: Land for Housing*, PPG3, London: DoE.

Department of Environment (1992b) *Competing for Quality in Housing*, London: DoE.

Department of Environment (1991a) *Household Projections*, London: DoE.

Department of Environment (1991b) *Circular 7/91: Planning and Affordable Housing*, London: HMSO.

Department of Environment (1988) *English House Condition Survey, 1986*, London: HMSO.

Department of Environment (1977) *Housing Policy: a Consultation Document*, cmnd 6551, London: HMSO.

Ermisch J (1990) (ed) *Housing and the National Economy*, Aldershot: Gower.

Greve J (1990) *Homelessness in Britain*, London: SHAC.

Hills J (1991) *Unravelling Housing Finance*, Oxford: Clarendon Press.

Kleinman M P (1991) A Decade of Change: Providing Social Housing 1980-1990, Discussion Paper 33, University of Cambridge: Department of Land Economy.

Kleinman M P and Whitehead C M E (1991) *London's Housing Needs*, London: LFHA.

Le Grand J and Robinson R (1984) (eds) *Privatisation and the Welfare State*, London: George Allen & Unwin.

London Planning Advisory Committee (1992) Housing and the Labour Market: London World City Report on Studies, Paper 1.9, London: LPAC.

London Planning Advisory Committee (1991) *London: World City*, London: HMSO.

London Planning Advisory Committee (1988) *Access to Housing in London: Report of Studies*, London: LPAC.

London Research Centre/Association of London Authorities (1987) *Greater London House Condition Survey 1985*, London: ALA.

London Research Centre (1991) *Housing Access and Affordability in Islington*, London: LRC.

London Research Centre (1990a) *London Housing Statistics 1989*, London: LRC.

London Research Centre (1990b) *Housing Need and the Supply of Social Rented Housing in London*, London: LRC.

London Research Centre (1990c) *Private Sector Leasing in London 1989*, London: LRC.

London Research Centre (1988) *Access to Housing in London*, London: LRC.

The London and South-East Regional Planning Conference (1990) *Access to Affordable Housing in the South-East*, London: SERPLAN.

Maclennan D and Williams R (1990) *Affordable Housing in Britain and America*, York: Joseph Rowntree Foundation.

National Federation of Housing Associations (1992) *Housing Associations after the Act*, London: NFHA.

Royal Institution of Chartered Surveyors (1992) *Living Cities*, London: The Royal Institution of Chartered Surveyors.

Whitehead C M E (1984) Privatisation and Housing, in Le Grand J and Robinson R (eds) *Privatisation and the Welfare State*, London: George Allen & Unwin.

Whitehead C M E and Cross D T (1991) Affordable Housing in London, *Progress and Planning*, **36** (1).

Whitehead C M E and Kleinman M P (1987) Private Renting in London: Is it so Different, *Journal of Social Policy*, **16** (3) (July 1987).

# 7 Education

*Donald Naismith*

## The national background

### *The problem*

There can be few more important things to people than the education they give to their children.  It must come high up on any 'quality of life' scale. Unfortunately, for over a decade there has been growing dissatisfaction, increasingly expressed, with our schools, not only in London, but in the country as a whole.

  In Britain the inquisition into the state of education began in earnest with the then Prime Minister, Jim Callaghan, making a speech at Ruskin College, Oxford in 1967.  In it he called for a 'Great Debate' on the educational issues of the day and said "You (the teachers) must satisfy the parents and industry that what you are doing meets their requirements and the needs of their children.  For if the public is not convinced then the profession will be laying trouble for itself in the future".  In America similar alarm bells were rung by the Commission of Excellence in Education's report, *A Nation at Risk* (1983).

  The causes of concern in both countries - as well as suggested remedies - are remarkably similar.  As far as causes are concerned these are: first, low educational expectations, attainments and training skills in relation to other countries, in particular, those of old adversaries: in the case of America, Japan, in the case of Britain, Germany.  The second cause is the greater value and esteem placed on the 'academic excellence' attainable by the few and the greater resources devoted to them; a cultural preference for abstract over applied learning; the low prestige of vocational education and training;

our failure to create a successful system of mass education in which all have equal opportunities to excel. The third cause is disillusionment with the teaching methods of the 1960s, in particular 'child-centred' learning in primary education - the emphasis on the role of play and individual enquiry at the expense of more didactic approaches involving teaching the whole class - a feeling that traditional basic knowledge and skills were undervalued and not taught; in secondary education, mixed-ability teaching in comprehensive schools disregarding the individual's abilities and aptitudes; the discouragement of competition. The fourth is uncertainty about the purpose and nature of education in both our increasingly multi-ethnic and multi-cultural societies - uncertainty, indeed, about what we mean by these terms -and the role government should play; uncertainty about the place of religious education in the system.

One powerful view of the position was brutally, however inaccurately, summed up for me during a visit to the United States by the phrase 'the bright, white flight'. In short, the white, Anglo-Saxon, middle classes, whenever they can do so, are deserting the nation's publicly-funded schools for private, independent schools which continue to maintain their personal values. I make no apology for casting what I have to say against an international background. Our cities are cosmopolitan in their make-up. Our children will have to find their way in an 'international' world. In the words of *A Nation at Risk* which belong to us all:

> *What was unimaginable a generation ago has begun to occur - others are matching and surpassing our educational attainments ... The world is indeed one global village. We live among determined, well-educated and strongly-motivated competitors. We compete with them for international standing and markets, not only with products, but also with the ideas of our laboratories and neighbourhood workshops. America's (Great Britain's) position in the world may once have been reasonably secure, with only a few excellently well-trained men and women. It is no longer.* (Commission of Excellence: 1983)

## Schools matter

Assessing the purpose and effectiveness of education has engaged the attention of civilised society since the time of Plato, no doubt before as well. It was certainly high on the agenda of the Inner London Education Authority (ILEA), which was responsible for inner London's education between 1965 and 1990. One of its most influential reports was published in 1988; called *Schools Matter*, the scope of its investigation can be readily seen from its aims:

> *The first was to produce a detailed description of pupils and teachers, and of the organisation and curriculum of the schools.*

*The second was to document the progress and development, over four years of schooling, of nearly 200 pupils. Our third and key aim was to establish whether some schools were more effective than others in promoting pupils' learning and development, once account had been taken of variations in the characteristics of pupils in the intakes to schools. The fourth was to investigate differences in the progress of different groups of pupils. Special attention was paid to achievement related to the race, sex and social class backgrounds of pupils. In addition, we wanted to examine the effects of differences of age on children's achievement. In order to pursue these aims, we addressed the following questions: Are some schools or classes more effective than others, when variations in the intakes of pupils are taken into account? Are some schools or classes more effective for particular groups of children? If some schools or classes are more effective than others, what factors contribute to these positive effects?* (ILEA: 1988)

It will come as no surprise that the conclusion of this impressive study was, as its name suggests, that schools do matter. The school your child goes to can make a real difference to his or her achievement whatever the variables.


*The 'sociological' approach*

At this point it is as well to say that one of the most significant characteristics underlying recent educational reforms in this country is the rejection of what I may call the 'sociological' approach, the idea that the *status quo* can be analysed and described in sociological terms and then improved by pulling this or that lever of public policy through a process of planning informed by sociological data. In other words 'social engineering' has gone out of the window. It didn't work in the past and there is no reason to suppose it will work in the future.

All of us are aware of the enormous volume of such information about education systems studies have yielded and the suggested nostrums which have arisen from them. Peter Mortimore in his 1991 lecture *Bucking the trends: promoting successful urban education*, provides a helpful and expert summary of internationally known projects aimed at improving standards in, as the title suggests, urban areas (Mortimore 1991). Among these are: first, early childhood programmes such as 'High Scope' (UK); second, school effectiveness programmes, for example the Canadian School Growth Plan, the Cromer Development Plan (USA), the OECD International Schools Improvement Project (14 nations); third, special programmes including the Education and Social Environment Project (The Netherlands), the Technical and Vocational Educational Initiative (UK), the Reading Recovery Project (New Zealand), the Cognitive Acceleration through Science Education Scheme (UK); fourth, school linked projects, examples include the Haringey Experiment (UK), Compact Schemes (USA); and fifth, new learning environments such as Meihan's flexi-schooling, and magnet schools (both USA).

Peter Mortimore enters two crucial caveats: first, evidence of their effectiveness judged in terms of either concurrent or long term outcomes is rarely available; and second:

> *those who have engaged with the close detail of policy and practice in urban education abstracted from wider issues have laid themselves open to the charge of producing naive school centred solutions with no sense of the structural, the political and the historical as constraints.* (Grace 1984)

The government has quite openly decided to do away with these constraints, to dispense in effect with the *status quo*, to cut through the sociological entanglements and to rest its strategy squarely on securing the effectiveness of schools through the operation of 'market forces'. Market forces, parent power, choice, in the government's view stand a better chance of producing better schools than attempting to influence the classic variables which are taken into account in considering education policy: the indices of social deprivation, large families, one-parent families, parental occupation, pupil behaviour, pupil mobility, ethnic background, fluency in English.

## The government's response

The government, however, is not interested in variables. In requiring schools to publish statistics about their performance, for instance, the government has insisted that raw scores only should be used and that attempts to qualify these by reference to social factors, for example, to give a 'value-added' assessment should remain an academic exercise.

The government is interested in certainties. There is no way, it has concluded, that educational policy could or should be dictated or influenced by sociological approaches, however well intentioned and scientifically founded, probably quite simply because it feels it has no control over such variables, and governments like to be in control. A more certain reason is that it feels that in education, as in many other areas of national life, government, whether central or local, is part of the problem not the solution. On this analysis many of the country's educational difficulties stem from the fact that schools are regarded as agents of inefficient, politically, if not ideologically, motivated and unrepresentative local government rather than as a service responding to individual parents' and pupils' needs and wishes.

The government has taken the view, therefore, that the only sure way to improve standards is to form an alliance with the parents, to adopt, in other words, the same approach it has adopted in other areas of public policy, namely, 'the customer knows best'. If schools give parents what they want, all will be well. But what do parents want? In 1989 the ILEA's Research and Statistics Branch reported that there were four important factors in parents' choosing of secondary schools: good discipline, the child's wishes, ease of access and good examination results (ILEA: 1989).

But this is, to some extent, beside the point. The fact is that whatever the results of the research, however well founded, the government has decided to sidestep the mass of analysis and adopt a direct 'consumerist' approach to public services. As it sees things the role of the government is to secure the public interest through ensuring quality by enforcing standards. Its job is to deal with the ends, the purpose of the enterprise, not the means, which can be left to a variety of - preferably competing - agencies. It does not matter whether this is water, energy, housing, health or transport.

## A 'Consumerist' approach to education

As far as education is concerned four consumers may be identified: the state (in which we may include employers), parents, pupils and the schools themselves. The state's interest can be met by a new national system of quality control. The interests of the parents and pupils can be met by a 'market' of self-governing schools which would, themselves, in addition to competing for pupils, be able to 'buy-in' those services needed to respond to their customers' wishes without the 'planning intervention' of local or central government.

Accordingly a system of 'quality control' safeguarding the state's interest has been created by the following measures: first, the introduction of a National Curriculum guaranteeing to all pupils a broad, balanced education, whichever school they go to; second, the introduction of a national system of assessment based on the re-establishment of standards of attainment (grades), openly indicating what may be expected of pupils at key stages of their development; third, the publication of test results and other performance indicators; and fourth, a new system of inspection, putting a greater distance between the government's and local authorities' (districts') inspectors and schools.

The 'market' for parents and pupils is to be created by widening the range of schools and making them more accessible through the following major reforms. First, opting out enables schools, if the governors and parents so wish, to leave local authority control and become self-governing, paid for directly by the government on much the same basis as those schools which choose to remain with the local authority. These schools are called grant-maintained schools. Free from the policies of their previous masters, the argument runs, such schools are likely to take on, chameleon-like, the characteristics looked for by their clientele, particularly in view of the second reform.

Second, the Local Management of Schools scheme whereby in future schools, whether grant-maintained or remaining within a local authority's responsibility, will be financed in the main on the basis of the numbers on roll. Under this scheme roughly 85 percent of all schools' income will depend on how many pupils they enrol. Through these means, it is argued, schools responding to the differing wishes of parents' wishes will flourish, those which do not will fail.

Third, as a contribution to a wider range of schools the government has created a completely new kind of school, the City Technology College. This is an independent school financed by employers and the government, offering a distinctive education in which emphasis is placed on science, technology, mathematics and on an understanding of industry and commerce.

Fourth, open enrolment removes the ability of local authorities to restrict the intake into popular, over-subscribed schools on 'planning' grounds, in other words allowing schools to admit to the full extent of their physical capacity. The government has announced changes to the way capital allocations are to be made, that is money needed for permanent improvements. Whereas before the overriding priority was to meet the basic needs of districts, to provide 'roofs over heads' in future 'popular' schools will attract additional funds to enable them to expand.

Accompanying these reforms is insistence that the public has access to better information about the performance of schools because without such information choice is blind. Under a government initiative known as the Citizens' Charter, schools, whether maintained by local or central government, are required to publish information about their performance, in particular their test and examination results, their attendance rates and in the case of secondary schools, the proportion of students who go on to further and higher education, training and employment.

All this will be readily recognisable to Americans as virtually identical to their government's 'choice' programme.


## London's position

### The background to change

An enormous amount of information is available to us about education in inner London as a result of the systematic and open study of schools and education undertaken by ILEA's Research and Statistics Branch. The tables in the Appendix to this chapter give a comprehensive overview of education in inner London in 1989.

They describe, however, a situation which the government found unacceptable. As a result the government added to the national changes already indicated the further major reform of transforming the way education has been provided and administered in the capital for over 100 years.

Until 1990 the way education was organised in inner London differed from every other part of the country where education was only one of a number of services provided by 'multi-purpose' elected councils. From 1870 education was the responsibility of a 'single-purpose' authority, first the London School Board, then under the London County Council, from

1965 the Inner London Education Authority. On 1st April 1990 responsibility for education was transferred from ILEA to the individual boroughs in inner London, so that education is provided there in the same way as education is provided in all other parts of the country namely, by local councils which are education authorities. The 13 boroughs are: Camden, the City of Westminster, Greenwich, Hackney, Hammersmith and Fulham, Islington, Kensington and Chelsea, Lambeth, Lewisham, Southwark, Tower Hamlets and Wandsworth. The City of London is not referred to in the tables in the Appendix as this district maintains only one (primary) school.

The principal reason given for the abolition of ILEA was that it was inefficient. In spite of the facts that it was a 'single purpose' authority and thereby able to channel all its resources in one direction, and that it was a 'precepting' authority, that is it raised the money it needed by levying contributions from member boroughs without effective restriction, it failed to deliver a satisfactory service which commanded public confidence. In the financial year 1988-89 the net expenditure per secondary pupil in ILEA was £2,505, making ILEA the highest spending of all the 96 local education authorities of England and Wales. The ratio of pupils to teacher, the Pupil Teacher Ratio (PTR) in ILEA in January 1990 was 18.8:1 in primary, and 14.8:1 in secondary schools. This was the most generous primary PTR in England and Wales, and the second most generous secondary PTR. The average class size in 1989 of ILEA primary schools was 21.6 pupils, and 19.6 in secondary schools.

Such high levels of spending and good teacher numbers and class sizes were not, however, reflected in acceptable standards of performance. Examination results at ages 16 and 18 were poor. In the summer of 1990, 20 percent of children in inner London left school without any graded GCSE result against 8 percent nation-wide (the General Certificate of Secondary Education examination (GCSE) is the main 'school-leavers'' examination at the end of compulsory schooling); 16 percent left with no passes at GCE A'level against 9.5 percent nationally (the General Certificate of Education (GCE) A'level is the main requirement for entry to higher education). Attendance at age 15 was low, averaging 74 percent. ILEA ranked 64th out of the 96 LEAs in England in terms of participation in post-16 education or training.

These results have to be seen, however, against the socially difficult circumstances shown in the high proportion of children claiming free meals, belonging to large or single-parent families, speaking a first language other than English, and whose parents were unemployed.

Furthermore, although ILEA could largely determine its revenue expenditure without too much interference, central government exercised the same tight control, as in the case of all other local authorities, over its capital expenditure, that is money needed for long-term improvements to building stock and equipment for which money has to be borrowed and repaid over time. There is no doubt that under-investment in buildings has led to very poor physical accommodation in many schools in London. One estimate puts the amount of money needed to bring all ILEA schools up to standard at £750 million.

Against this has to be put the argument that ILEA was slow to take out of use expensive empty places created by demographic trends, in particular, the fall in the birth rate in the mid-1960s. Between 1970 and 1989 the school population (ages 5-16) plummeted from 413,000 to 275,000, a decline of 34 percent.

A further, and in a way more serious, criticism was that ILEA had failed to do what only it could do as a 'single-purpose' authority, namely, to transfer resources from rich to poor areas, to smooth out the gross inequalities represented within its boundaries.

Supporters of ILEA appealed to a 'London factor' which argued that education in the inner boroughs should be managed on a unitary basis. It is doubtful if such a 'London factor' is at work. Again Peter Mortimore:

> *By aggregating (the country's) Local Education Authorities into three clusters of 'London', 'other metropolitan areas' and 'non-metropolitan areas', it is possible to show that in the non-metropolitan areas approximately 28 percent of school leavers have five higher grades in the public examinations in comparison to 23 percent of the leavers from London and the other metropolitan areas. However, since some non-metropolitan LEAs include sizeable cities and on the other hand some of the London boroughs and the metropolitan LEAs contain mainly suburbs - the 5 percent difference clearly marks enormous variation. In the thirteen inner and twenty outer London boroughs, for instance, stark contrasts occur between one LEA with only 11 percent of such school leavers and another with nearly 39 percent. Individual schools present an even greater range of achievements.* (Mortimore 1991)

And again the importance of the 'school factor'.

Clearly the abolition of ILEA in itself was a recognition that there was no 'London factor' which required education to be organised on a cross-borough basis.

In summary, there was, critics pointed out, no managerial link between the input of resources and the outcome of results. More important, not only was ILEA badly managed in the government's eyes, it demonstrated the inadequacy of local government generally to provide an effective education service.

Until the 1988 Education Reform Act the local authority was the main partner in the English education system. It controlled what was taught, the curriculum, and the resources schools needed. It employed the staff and provided the buildings, equipment and the supporting services. The Education Reform Act changed all that. It transferred responsibility for the curriculum upwards to central government, and sent down responsibility for the greater part of expenditure for the day to day running of schools to the schools themselves. In addition, under other legislation, all local authorities were required to put out many of their services to competitive tender, and plans are well advanced to remove all post-age 16 colleges from local authority control.

It is ironic that at the very time as the 13 new inner London education authorities were being created as an answer to London's problems, local authorities throughout the country were being effectively stripped of their powers.

It is important to recognise, therefore, that the clout of the local education authority is now extremely limited. Educational improvements in London and elsewhere necessarily depend heavily on national policies to a greater degree than ever before.

## One borough's response: Wandsworth's

Nonetheless, to get some idea of the changing scene of education in London, how the new boroughs are reshaping the education service in their districts, and to try to see things from the point of view of the new consumers, let us look at education in one borough, Wandsworth. As the largest of the inner London boroughs with a population of 260,000, containing widely differing communities, it is representative, as can be seen from an examination of the Appendix, to some degree, of the characteristics and issues belonging to all boroughs. And a look at Wandsworth is particularly relevant because, under Conservative control, it takes a 'consumerist' view of policy.

Wandsworth was the first of the inner London boroughs to argue that it should take over education in its area. Although there was a strong campaign to save ILEA, there is little support now to bring it back in any further reorganisation of local government in London which a future government may wish to consider. It has already been shown that the smaller, directly-elected councils are better able to manage the education service and to get to grips with their own problems, quite simply because they are nearer to them, politicians are more accountable and people naturally impatient of inaction. ILEA was far too large to be sufficiently responsive to local circumstances. In addition it was ideologically wedded to ideals of egalitarianism which prompted it to seek the same solutions for widely varying problems and which impeded much needed change in very differing areas.

By and large those inner London councils which are controlled by the Labour Party have tended to stay with the basic pattern of education they inherited from ILEA which, for the greatest part of its time, was itself Labour in political complexion. In particular they have remained with the concept of education as a 'supply-led' planned system with neighbourhood (zoned) comprehensive schools constituting a virtual monopoly. Changes have tended to restrict themselves to two reforms: first, replacing the sixth form, that is the two years 16-18+ in secondary schools catering for the 11-18 age range, by more broadly-based post-16 'tertiary colleges' more geared up to part-time as well as full-time students and those following 'vocational' as well as those following 'academic' courses; second, relaxing ILEA's policies of controlling the intake to comprehensive schools in such a way as to attempt to ensure that every school's student population represents a cross-section of the ability range.

Those councils which are Conservative controlled have tended to take wider advantage of their new-found powers to embark on more radical change. Wandsworth is no exception. Its policies towards education and other public services are directed at creating a 'demand-led' system, at widening choice and encouraging competition. In these ways, it argues, standards will rise and efficiency improve.

*Primary education*

Wandsworth's primary (ages 5-11) and its secondary (ages 11-16) school populations are 17,000 and 6,880 respectively. It is unlikely that these will change significantly over the next decade. Because administratively Wandsworth is only one part of a highly compact conurbation, pupils move across its boundaries into and outside the borough for their education for a variety of reasons, proximity naturally being among the most prevalent.

Wandsworth maintains 51 'county' and 19 'voluntary' primary schools. 'County' schools are schools wholly owned, maintained and managed by the local council. 'Voluntary' schools are denominational - Anglican or Roman Catholic - provided and maintained jointly by the church authorities and the council. Three schools are divided into separate infant (ages 5-8) and junior (ages 8-11) departments. It is the council's policy that such schools should be amalgamated wherever circumstances exist to provide all-through education from ages 5-11.

It is also the council's policy that primary schools should be able to cater for at least 180 and preferably 360 pupils. In Wandsworth's view only schools of this size can provide the balanced and differentiated programme of learning required by the National Curriculum and can be financially viable and properly staffed under the Local Management of Schools scheme.

The buildings of most primary schools date from Victorian times or from the 1960s, both periods of rapid population expansion. Many are in need of substantial improvements.

In primary education in Wandsworth there have been three major developments. The first is the introduction of comprehensive nursery (ages three to five) education available to all those parents who want it. There is a part-time place for every three year-old and a full-time place for every four year-old.

This generous if not unique level of provision has been made possible by taking advantage of, first, diverting from the Social Services Department under-used 'child-care' arrangements in which children are cared for 'socially' but are not taught 'educationally', and second, some of the surplus places in primary schools amounting to almost 9,000 left by a declining school population.

Bringing the resources of the council's Social Services and Education Departments together to such good effect was not possible before 1990 because of the divided responsibilities between ILEA and Wandsworth, and is a good example of one of the benefits of local government reform in London.

Under-five childcare and education arrangements are extremely varied. Voluntary and private organisations all have an important part to play. The Education Department is considering the introduction of vouchers as a means of enhancing parental choice, effectively bringing together the differing and changing needs of families with children at this age and the multiplicity of agencies available to them.

The second development is a re-think about the purpose and nature of primary schools. The post-war public education system was organised into three distinctive and largely self-contained phases, primary (5-11), secondary (11-16) and further (16+). These, it was considered, reflected the main stages of a young person's development. This concept has been challenged by the introduction, through the National Curriculum, of levels of attainment or grades, as they would be called in the United States, independent of age. As a result, Wandsworth wishes to see primary schools to be more 'preparatory' in terms of secondary education in future.

The third development is the establishment of two French schools, *écoles maternelles*, occupying spare accommodation in primary schools, French in every respect in terms of teaching and lessons, the lessons running in parallel with those of their hosts' English schools; an interesting manifestation of the changing institutional life of the capital city responding to the needs of its cosmopolitan population.


*Primary standards*

One of the main reasons for giving Wandsworth, along with the other boroughs, responsibility for education was to raise standards across the board but particularly in literacy and numeracy. More information exists about literacy than numeracy. An examination was conducted of performance of Wandsworth primary schools in 1990, against two determinants: reading performance as measured by the London Reading Test which assesses comprehension, and the proportion of children claiming school meals, a reliable indicator of social deprivation commonly accepted as perhaps the single most influential factor in a child's performance. The results strongly indicate that the way a school is run can be a more powerful determinant of performance, measured in this way, than either ethnic or social background.

*Secondary education*

As far as secondary education is concerned Wandsworth faced three issues: the need to reduce the number of surplus school places it inherited - approximately 4,500; at the same time, the contradictory aim of widening parental and pupil choice through introducing a better range of different kinds of school; third, whether to reorganise the pattern of post-16 education. Although all its county schools were geared up to cater for the 11-18 age range, most of their 'sixth forms' covering the two years from 16-18 years were no longer viable because of the fall in school population, a consequential unattractive, narrow range of subject opportunities, and better choice and more adult conditions in 'tertiary' or further education colleges.

Wandsworth's response was first, to close two single-sex schools, one all-boys' and the other all-girls', leaving a stronger school of each kind within the system to be retained; second, to support the establishment of a City Technology College; third, to support the establishment of an Anglican secondary school to meet the needs of about 1,000 Wandsworth pupils who had to seek such a denominational education outside the borough which had no Church of England secondary school (the Roman Catholic authorities had already re-organised their system to provide, in Wandsworth, two 11-16 schools and a sixth-form college); fourth, to support the application of schools wishing to opt out; fifth, to encourage a high degree of specialisation in three county schools, enabling them to concentrate on a curricular theme or focus supported by facilities and levels of tuition which cannot be replicated in other schools - to create, in American terminology, 'magnet' schools; sixth, to convert a failing 'down-town' comprehensive school into a selective Technology College; finally, to invite county schools to reconsider their 'comprehensive', that is, non-selective, nature and to undertake responsibility for their own admission procedures which are at the moment centralised in the Town Hall.

In this way, Wandsworth considers that it can break up the almost monopolistic dependence of the previous system on the neighbourhood comprehensive school which was a mainstay of ILEA's policy. The underlying assumptions of the neighbourhood comprehensive system are: first, that one school can cater for the needs of all children; second, that the intake of such schools should be determined largely by proximity and by a system of allocation by the council aimed at ensuring a 'balanced' intake distributed among three bands of ability; and third, that the predominant method of teaching should be along mixed-ability lines.

Wandsworth quarrels with all three assumptions. It believes that children, as they grow up in different ways, need access to different schools. It believes that parents should be able to choose the school most appropriate to their children and not have this decision made for them on grounds of financial efficiency or social engineering. It also believes that children should be enabled to progress through their learning at their own pace and not be held back by organisational considerations based solely on age or the real or imagined benefits of 'social mix'.

Although the internal organisation of schools is properly a matter for the schools themselves, Wandsworth discourages mixed-ability teaching. It is interested in encouraging 'tracking' in the sense it is used in some parts of America to mean organising a school in such a way as to enable students to 'negotiate' their own timetable, subject by subject, according to their demonstrable strengths. Such a method powerfully enhances the student's capacity as consumer, in charge of his or her own education.

A main aim of policy is to compete for pupils, to attract back to Wandsworth's secondary schools a large proportion of those parents who have been seeking an education for their children elsewhere. Between 1974 and 1989, after taking account of the effects of the fall in school population, numbers of pupils equivalent of two large secondary schools sought their education outside the local system. The flight might not have been white or bright, but flight it certainly was. In 1990, 20 percent of all resident pupils found their education in independent schools; another 20 percent went outside the borough, although these were compensated for by a similar proportion of children coming in from other boroughs, the two migratory batches belonging to a wider movement of population from inner London to the generally more socially desirable outer London areas; a ripple from the centre to the periphery, from east to west. There is evidence that the tide has turned. Figures of first preferences for Wandsworth's schools over the past three years show, in each case, a net gain.

*Secondary standards*

Early results are encouraging. At age 16, the proportion of the year group leaving school without any GCSE accreditation has been reduced by one third over the last three years from 19 percent in 1989 to 13 percent in 1991 against an inner London average of 18 percent and a national average of 8 percent. The proportion of pupils obtaining five or more GCSE passes between grades A and C (within a range from A to E) has increased from 17 percent in 1989 to 25 percent in 1991 against an inner London average of 20 percent and a national average of 32 percent.

At age 18, the proportion of pupils obtaining at least one GCE A'level pass has increased from 61 percent in 1989 to 63.5 percent in 1990 and 69 percent in 1991, moving towards the national average of 77 percent. The proportion of passes graded A to C has increased from 34.5 percent in 1989 to 39 percent in 1991. One can go on and on in this vein.

Of course such over-simplified results tell only part of the story and mask many of the sociological factors at work.

*The ethnic dimension*

The extent of the ethnicity of Wandsworth is apparent from the statistics accompanying this paper. The importance of good race relations is a main feature of council policy. There is regular dialogue with ethnic community representatives. Equal opportunity policies are taken seriously. Many aspects of the public services, employment, school attendance rates and examination results, for example, are monitored on an ethnic basis. Relations between the communities in schools are considered to be good.

Although the process of integration - however this word is used - is, on the whole, well handled and successful, there are three recurring claims which, it has to be said, are not satisfactorily met. These are first, that the teaching force and the administration of the education service including the governors of schools do not reflect the ethnic composition of society; second, children from Afro-Caribbean backgrounds who make up some 18 percent of the population under achieve and are alienated from school culture, so much so that supplementary schools are needed; third, that the Muslim community which represents a majority of the Asian school population, about 12 percent of the total, should have their own schools in much the same way as the Anglican and the Roman Catholic communities have their own schools, a claim sharpened by recent legislation emphasising the predominantly Christian nature of the religious worship which must take place each day.

Most education authorities seek to meet the first two through specific measures. The third, however, presents a more serious challenge. The fear is that Muslim schools would impede progress towards the homogeneous society many assume to be the purpose of 'integration' and indeed one of the purposes of the education system itself.

Applications to establish Muslim schools have been turned down on the grounds that while surplus places exist, as is the case in many parts of the country, the expense of additional schools cannot be justified. The increased powers of the governors of schools and the introduction of grant maintained schools have produced means whereby Muslim groups in predominantly Muslim areas are able to exercise considerable influence, if not control, over the management of schools, although such schools must teach the National Curriculum and practise equal opportunity policies between the sexes. There is evidence to suggest that although pressure for denominational Muslim schools comes from parents, children prefer to take their place in local schools with their friends from other communities.

To meet specific needs arising from the multi-ethnic nature of society, very considerable sums of money are allocated each year by central government. Wandsworth's allocation for 1992-93 amounts to £2.8 million.

*Specific grants*

Such specific grants belong to a wider programme of project-led initiatives financed by central government to meet closely defined needs and for which local authorities are invited to bid. In revenue terms, in addition to those already mentioned, the most prominent are those aimed at teacher in-service training and promoting curricular initiatives.

In capital terms allocations are also made available under a whole range of headings usually associated with curricular developments - the Schools Technology Initiative is the most recent example - for improving the environment and enhancing facilities in areas of physical dereliction.

These central government aid programmes have grown in size and significance in recent years. They clearly fly in the face of the government's underlying strategy of reliance on formula funding which underpins most of local government finance and that of schools and its faith in its market prospectus. Perhaps the 'sociological' approach still lives!

*Continuing education*

Another main aim of Wandsworth's education policies is to encourage pupils to continue their education, either on a full- or part-time basis in further and then on to higher education or to take up training whether in or out of employment. The proportion of the age cohort doing so increased from 62 percent in 1989-90 to 69 percent in 1991-92. Part of this is, of course, due to the economic recession. But without a commitment to continuous education and training, there is little chance of individuals improving their employment prospects or the country producing the skilled workforce it plainly needs.

Most young people who do not want to stay on at school at age 16 go on to a college of further education. There are two in Wandsworth. Their main job is to provide a wide range of 'academic' and 'vocational' courses for young people, mainly between the ages of 16 and 25.

The government has already gone a long way to break down the damaging cultural barrier between academic and vocational courses. The 'vocationalisation' of the education system has begun. Courses leading to vocational qualifications are being introduced in increasing numbers into schools for pupils at age 14. Of particular importance is the establishment of the National Council for Vocational Qualifications. Its task is to bring together the many separate qualifications which have grown up over the years in different trades, professions and businesses into a coherent framework of qualifications, in which common values recognising five levels of competence to university pass degree standard are put into currency. The government's decision to remove the distinction between polytechnics and universities will give powerful institutional reinforcement to the movement towards a comprehensive system of further and higher education.

At this point it may be helpful to refer to the pattern of higher education in inner London, that is the education offered in universities, polytechnics and institutions of further and higher education.

Higher education is, as one would expect, well represented in inner London.   There are two existing universities: the massive University of London itself comprising 40 colleges, schools and institutes with some 90,000 students, and the City University with 4,000 students.   Five former polytechnics cater for 47,000 students and are joined by seven Higher Education Colleges offering specialist studies in speech and drama, art and design, teacher training, music and nursing.   It is important to realise, however, that in this country institutions of higher education are meant to meet national and regional needs.   It would be wrong to imagine that the institutions described primarily serve the geographical area of inner London.

In spite of attempts to establish close links between local schools and Colleges of Further Education through the development of transferable credits, entry to higher education remains highly competitive with many casualties.   Some people would like to see institutions of higher education serve their more immediate localities to reduce the cost of residential arrangements and to facilitate an easier progression to degree level work on the basis of entitlement.

The introduction of training vouchers nationally, enabling students to buy the courses most suited to their needs (compare with the examination being undertaken in Wandsworth of their application to pre-five year-old care and education) should not be under-rated in the movement towards giving freer access to courses the students themselves choose.   Valuable though such measures are, what is not yet firmly rooted in the system however, is the concept of education as a life-long entitlement.   Although lip-service is paid to the ideal of education as a 'ladder of opportunity', the necessary institutional arrangements are not yet comprehensively in place. What is needed is acceptance of the idea that success at one educational stage entitles the student access to the next.   In addition to being a powerful motivator, it puts students as consumers in charge of their own education.

The concept of education as a life-long entitlement has found nowhere a more forcible expression than in 'adult education', until recently the umbrella phrase signifying access to literally every kind of course anyone might seek at any one time, either for recreation or as compensatory learning.   Adult education was one of ILEA's greatest achievements. Although critics will point to its high degree of financial subsidy, no less than 250,000 people used its services each year.

Unfortunately dangers to adult education come from two directions. Locally it is highly unlikely that the successor inner London boroughs can continue traditionally high degrees of subsidy amounting to, in some respects, 80 percent.   Nationally, the government is redefining adult education more narrowly and putting it on a less secure institutional footing.

*Special education*

To no group is effective access to the education system of more particular importance than to people with learning difficulties, children with special educational needs. It is estimated that one in five children will need specific help at some point in their time at school. Provision for special education in London is good. In addition to the highly specialist schools for those with severe physical or behavioural difficulties, a wide range of support is available through the Schools Psychological Service and related agencies.

Parents of children from the age of two who might be showing signs of learning difficulty have the right to have their child examined. The public authorities are under a duty to provide corrective action if this is required. In school terms, where it is decided such specific help is needed parents are provided with a 'statement' indicating the nature of the problem and what is being done to put it right or improve matters. In all authorities there will be agreement that there is scope for improvement in two respects: all children should be diagnosed more quickly, and more resources should be made available for providing the support and treatment identified. 'Statementing' often takes a long time, largely because of the involvement of so many specialists, and the difficulty of reaching professional and parental agreement about what should be done. One proposal to speed up the process is to allow parents to secure statements from their own professional advisers rather than depend on the local authority's educational psychologists, often suspected of being too closely associated with the local authority's concern to keep costs down in a very expensive area of activity.

In recent times there has been growing support to integrate children with special educational needs into 'mainstream' schooling. There are, however, unfortunate signs that now that schools are in charge of their own expenditure and greater emphasis is being placed on performance, children with special needs are no longer as welcome as they were in schools regrettably anxious to remove what they may see as complications in the way of getting other pupils through their grades and their school moving up the league table.

A similar phenomenon is beginning to be experienced in schools' attitude to troublesome children. There has been a sharp rise in the number of expulsions from schools. More worryingly, this includes a seemingly disproportionate increase in the number of children of Afro-Caribbean origin.


*Support services*

Three other invaluable support groups should be mentioned: the Education Welfare Service, the Careers Service and Inspection and Advice.

Education Welfare Service officers have, as one of their main tasks, following up truancy and trying to deal with its root causes. For obvious reasons increasing importance is being given to school attendance. The peak age for crime is 15. The figure speaks for itself. The real answer, of course, lies, not in better policing or social work, but in motivation at school.

The Careers Service advises youngsters on careers opportunities and tries to find jobs for them where they can. It is a valued service. Twenty-thousand young people used the service in Wandsworth last year.

Although these support services, the Educational Psychologists, the Education Welfare officers and the Careers Service are intrinsic to a good education service, there is increasing debate about whether they should be provided solely by the council. Is there not a case, it is argued, for floating them off into some kind of privatised arrangement, reinforcing the role of schools as consumers? Why should schools not, the question is being asked, buy in such services as they themselves wish rather than have to depend on publicly provided monopolies? Building and grounds maintenance, school meals, cleaning and transport have been put out to public competition. It may be claimed that there are no functions presently undertaken by local authorities which cannot be undertaken by other agencies. The prospect arises, therefore, of the schools as consumers buying in from a market of competing services those it considers most relevant to its circumstances.

This argument is being extended to Inspection and Advice. All local authorities maintain inspectors and advisers to monitor the performance of schools and to help with career and curricular development. One of the main aims of the government's plans for the reform of the national inspectorate, Her Majesty's Inspectorate, is to break, at national and local level, what is seen as the too cosy relationship between the 'education establishment' and schools which has grown up. In the government's view, the provider of whatever goods or services should not assess itself. Independent judgement relating to schools will be secured only if there is a distance between the institution and its inspection arrangements. Such a distance is to be secured under the government's reforms whereby schools and colleges will be inspected by government-approved specialists in accordance with a national programme.

*The teachers*

While all this is going on, of course, children have to be taught. What is the position relating to the teachers?

For many years concern was expressed about the adequacy of the number of teachers employed and whether their qualifications matched the subjects they were timetabled to teach. For a variety of reasons, most no doubt connected to the state of the labour market, the teacher supply situation has recently shown signs of improvement nationally with London showing the biggest improvement over the previous year. Although there are posts not permanently filled, all schools throughout the inner London area have sufficient teachers to maintain the timetable.

Two key aspects to teacher supply and morale often cited as being in a shaky position are professionalism and pay. So far the government has not supported the idea of the establishment of a teachers' council similar to the Law Society or the British Medical Association which look after the interests of their members and supervises their conduct and which are often regarded as marks of their status and professionalism. But it has established a Review Body along the lines of the organisations which decide the pay of civil servants, judges, generals, doctors, nurses and dentists. In this way it is intended to place pay negotiations for teachers on a more professional footing than the previous negotiating machinery which had existed since 1945 between the teacher unions, the local authorities (the employers) and the government (the ultimate paymaster).

The government is, however, keeping warm the idea that employers, whether local education authorities or governing bodies, should decide their own pay scales. It is deterred from this by the inflationary effects of possible leap-frogging settlements, and schools and areas lurching from feast to famine. But the idea remains a live one, if for no other reason that it would further seriously weaken trade union power. There exists considerable scope within a school's new powers for variation in teachers' salaries. One interesting idea is that part of pay settlements should be available to the staff of a school as a team in recognition of demonstrable improvement in the effectiveness of the school as a whole. The question of linking individual teachers' pay to performance is being met head-on for the first time. In this, appraisal understandably plays a crucial role.

All teachers and headteachers are now required to take part in appraisal arrangements aimed at ensuring that all teachers and headteachers are appraised once every two years. The components of appraisal are expected to include classroom observation, an interview, the preparation of an appraisal statement which may include performance targets and a follow-up.

Not surprisingly, an unresolved tension exists between those who see teacher appraisal principally concerned with the enhancement of a teacher's effectiveness and career development, and those who put at the heart of appraisal the effectiveness of the teacher as measured by demonstrable success on the part of the pupil.

## The government's programme

It will be clear from the foregoing that the English education system is being transformed, if not turned on its head. The aims of the government's reforms are fourfold. One aim is to create a wide variety of schools matching the differing needs of children; through this extension of parental and pupil choice standards in achievement, attendance and motivation will rise and the public monopoly of the neighbourhood comprehensive school will be broken. In this way, the interests of the parent as the consumer will be secured;

Second, the reforms aim to create an ideological framework whereby through the rehabilitation of selection, specialisation, differentiation, emphasis on progression, the introduction of grades independent of age, discouragement of mixed-ability teaching, the learning offered to pupils will be more closely attuned to their individual abilities, interests and strengths; in this way the interests of the pupils as consumer will be secured.

A third aim is to empower schools to have greater control over their management so that with the privatisation of Town Hall services they can compete for services as well as pupils on their own terms; in this way the interests of the school as consumer will be secured.

A fourth reform is to put in place a system of national quality control through the National Curriculum, standardised tests, the publication of performance indicators and a reformed inspectorate; in this way the interests of the state as consumer will be secured.

## Difficulties in the way

There are, however, a number of serious difficulties with this 'market' approach. One is that such an approach directly conflicts with the way the education system is financed, which is 'number sensitive'. Pressure is put on local government by central government to take 'uneconomic' 'surplus places' (that is, under-used school places brought about by demographic trends or unpopularity) out of use through closure and amalgamation. Such measures, however, by their very nature reduce variety and choice and reinforce the remaining system often most in need of the benefits of competition. In Wandsworth it would be difficult, if not impossible, for the council to establish, for example, a junior City Technology College for pupils between the ages of 8 and 11, which it wishes to do, because of the surplus of places. Similarly any plans for a Muslim school would run into the same difficulties.

In such a system, where the supply of school places is expected to be brought into correspondence with demand for reasons of financial efficiency, a market in the real sense cannot be said to exist. In a true market, the customer can take his or her business elsewhere. This is not the situation in prospect. The danger is that it will be the school which chooses the pupil, not the parent the school, the very reverse of the intentions of government policy. A means must therefore be found of empowering parents to have access to the education they wish for their children.

A second difficulty is that because there is no effective mechanism for rapidly and easily changing the pattern of education the range of different schools the government wishes to see will not come about of its own accord. There are only 15 City Technology Colleges out of a total of 4,000 maintained secondary schools, the overwhelming proportion, 90 percent of which are comprehensive.

The eventual decision whether a school should open, close or significantly change its character rests with the provider, in the broadest sense the Secretary of State for Education. Whoever holds this position controls the degree of variety and choice available. In addition, the legal procedures whereby schools can close, open, or change their character are lengthy, drawn out, complicated and openly hostile to change. More responsive routes, therefore, need to be found to enable a genuine variety of schools to be created. Furthermore, it is necessary to spell out which kinds of schools are meant to constitute variety. A more clearly articulated alternative to the neighbourhood comprehensive school is needed.

Third, the government's attitude towards failing schools is unclear. Whatever one's preference for the market as opposed to planning as a means of matching supply to demand for the very best of financial and educational reasons, it is patently unacceptable that the education of many children should depend on the random working of such a system.

Finally, no new sums of real money which the service needs will be generated. The system remains essentially a tightly-controlled 'top-down', 'supply-led' one, heavily dependent on planning mechanisms and considerations of arithmetic in terms of money tied to pupils.


**Ways forward**

I suggest that the following measures will need to be examined if the government's objectives are to be met. First, the system of financing education should be changed and surplus places regarded as an asset and not a liability. The education system should become 'demand-led'. All schools should be financed through fee-paying, and the amount of money the state now raises to finance education, which is unfairly distributed, should be transferred to the parents through tax credits so that they can pay or contribute to the education they want for their children; at a stroke this would remove the fatal divorce in this country between public and private education.

Second, whether a school opens, closes or undergoes a significant change in character should be a matter for the promoters or the governors of the school, subject to the school complying with national criteria relating to, for example, the requirements of the National Curriculum, the qualifications of staff, the soundness of management and compliance with building regulations. The role of the Secretary of State would be restricted to ensuring that these criteria are met.

In this way parents would have an escape route from the situation they may find themselves in living either in an area where the schools are unacceptably bad or where the schools are over subscribed and they cannot get their children in.

Third, a clear statement should be made about the kinds of school which will in future constitute the majority of schools providing the public system. Whatever form this definition takes, it is suggested that all parents should have reasonable access to first, selective schools geared up to the aptitudes and abilities of pupils suited to an 'academic' education; second, selective schools geared up to the   aptitudes and abilities of pupils suited to 'technological' education; and third, non-selective schools.  In addition there may be, where demand so exists, denominational schools and specialist schools concentrating, for example, on foreign languages or the performing arts and offering levels of tuition and facilities it is not possible to replicate in every school.

Fourth, to safeguard children against the free-fall of failing  schools, inspectors should be given similar powers to those in other parts of national life, namely requiring specific improvements to be made within defined times or penalties incurred or the school closed in the absence of satisfactory corrective action.  Whether a school is failing or not would be apparent from the annual scrutiny of performance indicators.

Finally, the question of the tenure of teachers should be tackled.  More flexibility should be introduced into the terms and conditions under which teachers, particularly headteachers, are employed.  It must be made easier to remove unsatisfactory teachers and headteachers.  Heavier emphasis in contracts should be placed on competence.  Arrangements for removal should be streamlined and fixed-term contracts encouraged.  Present arrangements form a main obstacle to beneficial change.

## The issues

Whatever one's view of the government's approach, it has at least reminded everyone that the responsibility for educating children in the modern state, regardless of the heavy and complex demands placed on it, remains that of the parent.  The central issues of the 1990s are: first, how far can and should we rely on the state to determine the kind of education parents may have for their children and the kind of education children wish for themselves without endangering the state's own legitimate stake in the education system; and second, whether through treating all the various people and institutions concerned, parents, pupils, schools, the state itself quite openly as consumers their interests can best be served through being brought fruitfully and harmoniously together in a civilised market.

## References

Grace G (1984) *Education in the City*, London: Routledge and Kegan Paul.

Commission of Excellence in Education's report (1983) *A Nation at Risk*, Washington: National Foundation for Education.

Mortimore P (1991) *Bucking the Trends: Promoting Successful Urban Education*, Times Educational Supplement/Greenwich Education Lecture.

ILEA Research and Statistics Branch (1989) *Which School? A study of parents' choice of secondary school*, 1230/89, London; Inner London Education Authority.

ILEA (1988) *Schools Matter*, London: Inner London Education Authority.

## Appendix
## Education in inner London in 1989

### Table 1
### Parental occupation : Primary pupils 1989

| Borough | Parental occupation | | | | | |
|---|---|---|---|---|---|---|
| | Non-manual % | Skilled manual % | Semi/ unskilled manual % | No wage earner % | Parents absent % | Unknown occupation % |
| Hammersmith & Fulham | 22.4 | 22.4 | 25.9 | 24.5 | 1.0 | 3.9 |
| Kensington & Chelsea | 28.8 | 17.1 | 27.1 | 20.6 | 1.2 | 5.3 |
| Westminster | 20.0 | 18.3 | 24.9 | 32.1 | 0.7 | 3.9 |
| Camden | 31.0 | 17.9 | 22.6 | 22.8 | 0.9 | 4.9 |
| Islington | 24.6 | 20.2 | 24.7 | 23.5 | 1.7 | 5.4 |
| Hackney | 17.1 | 17.0 | 23.7 | 34.7 | 0.7 | 6.8 |
| Tower Hamlets | 8.4 | 11.2 | 30.5 | 44.4 | 0.7 | 4.9 |
| Greenwich | 23.4 | 23.0 | 23.5 | 22.1 | 0.7 | 7.3 |
| Lewisham | 29.0 | 25.6 | 19.5 | 18.5 | 0.9 | 6.5 |
| Southwark | 19.7 | 18.1 | 23.7 | 30.2 | 1.2 | 7.2 |
| Lambeth | 24.4 | 16.6 | 21.3 | 28.0 | 1.3 | 8.4 |
| Wandsworth | 29.6 | 23.6 | 20.9 | 19.7 | 1.5 | 4.7 |
| All boroughs | 22.8 | 19.4 | 23.6 | 27.0 | 1.0 | 6.1 |

### Table 2
### Parental occupation : Secondary pupils 1989

| Borough | Parental occupation | | | | | |
|---|---|---|---|---|---|---|
| | Non-manual % | Skilled manual % | Semi/ unskilled manual % | No wage earner % | Parents absent % | Unknown occupation % |
| Hammersmith & Fulham | 22.2 | 20.5 | 24.1 | 18.4 | 2.8 | 11.9 |
| Kensington & Chelsea | 24.3 | 25.0 | 25.6 | 16.3 | 1.6 | 7.3 |
| Westminster | 30.3 | 22.8 | 18.3 | 25.6 | 0.6 | 2.5 |
| Camden | 37.6 | 22.3 | 15.9 | 16.6 | 0.9 | 6.7 |
| Islington | 16.0 | 20.1 | 29.4 | 22.1 | 3.6 | 8.8 |
| Hackney | 13.3 | 19.3 | 27.1 | 26.0 | 2.8 | 11.5 |
| Tower Hamlets | 8.9 | 17.8 | 23.8 | 35.9 | 1.2 | 12.4 |
| Greenwich | 23.7 | 22.7 | 17.7 | 13.4 | 1.1 | 21.3 |
| Lewisham | 24.1 | 24.6 | 20.3 | 13.4 | 2.1 | 15.5 |
| Southwark | 13.7 | 21.4 | 25.3 | 24.5 | 1.5 | 13.6 |
| Lambeth | 22.0 | 24.0 | 20.8 | 22.8 | 1.4 | 8.9 |
| Wandsworth | 20.8 | 25.0 | 25.7 | 18.1 | 1.9 | 8.4 |
| All boroughs | 21.3 | 22.2 | 22.3 | 20.7 | 1.7 | 11.8 |

Table 3
**Free meals : percentage of pupils eligible for free meals**

| Borough | All primary | Secondary |
|---|---|---|
| Hammersmith & Fulham | 46.0 | 45.7 |
| Kensington & Chelsea | 44.0 | 42.8 |
| Westminster | 49.4 | 50.9 |
| Camden | 45.8 | 39.0 |
| Islington | 47.1 | 55.7 |
| Hackney | 59.0 | 57.2 |
| Tower Hamlets | 72.5 | 67.7 |
| Greenwich | 38.1 | 32.3 |
| Lewisham | 37.9 | 37.3 |
| Southwark | 49.8 | 51.7 |
| Lambeth | 49.7 | 42.2 |
| Wandsworth | 41.4 | 43.4 |
| All boroughs | 48.6 | 46.2 |

Table 4
**Large families : percentage of pupils from families of 4+ children**

| Borough | All primary | Secondary |
|---|---|---|
| Hammersmith & Fulham | 20.4 | 26.8 |
| Kensington & Chelsea | 15.5 | 23.3 |
| Westminster | 22.2 | 25.7 |
| Camden | 21.8 | 17.5 |
| Islington | 20.5 | 29.4 |
| Hackney | 26.9 | 33.2 |
| Tower Hamlets | 45.7 | 43.0 |
| Greenwich | 17.9 | 19.4 |
| Lewisham | 16.3 | 23.9 |
| Southwark | 20.3 | 23.3 |
| Lambeth | 22.6 | 29.0 |
| Wandsworth | 20.5 | 26.1 |
| All boroughs | 22.9 | 26.4 |

Table 5

**One parent families : percentage of pupils from single parent families**

| Borough | All primary | Secondary |
|---|---|---|
| Hammersmith & Fulham | 32.5 | 32.2 |
| Kensington & Chelsea | 28.1 | 27.1 |
| Westminster | 30.0 | 31.5 |
| Camden | 25.7 | 28.6 |
| Islington | 30.4 | 33.8 |
| Hackney | 32.7 | 31.6 |
| Tower Hamlets | 20.5 | 22.2 |
| Greenwich | 22.9 | 21.7 |
| Lewisham | 25.6 | 28.7 |
| Southwark | 31.4 | 33.7 |
| Lambeth | 36.0 | 32.7 |
| Wandsworth | 28.2 | 32.4 |
| All boroughs | 28.4 | 29.2 |

Table 6

**Language : percentage of pupils who speak a language other than English at home**

| Borough | All primary | Secondary |
|---|---|---|
| Hammersmith & Fulham | 22.8 | 20.2 |
| Kensington & Chelsea | 35.2 | 35.9 |
| Westminster | 38.2 | 29.8 |
| Camden | 31.4 | 24.3 |
| Islington | 27.3 | 33.1 |
| Hackney | 35.0 | 33.8 |
| Tower Hamlets | 50.0 | 43.2 |
| Greenwich | 13.3 | 9.0 |
| Lewisham | 11.4 | 10.3 |
| Southwark | 17.7 | 18.9 |
| Lambeth | 17.9 | 23.4 |
| Wandsworth | 20.6 | 21.4 |
| All boroughs | 24.9 | 23.4 |

Table 7

Language : percentage of pupils not fluent in English

| Borough | All primary | Secondary |
|---------|-------------|-----------|
| Hammersmith & Fulham | 14.0 | 6.3 |
| Kensington & Chelsea | 22.5 | 16.9 |
| Westminster | 25.3 | 9.8 |
| Camden | 19.5 | 9.6 |
| Islington | 18.5 | 15.1 |
| Hackney | 25.1 | 17.3 |
| Tower Hamlets | 44.2 | 31.2 |
| Greenwich | 9.4 | 3.5 |
| Lewisham | 5.9 | 3.2 |
| Southwark | 11.0 | 6.1 |
| Lambeth | 11.0 | 10.0 |
| Wandsworth | 12.4 | 4.8 |
| All boroughs | 17.2 | 10.2 |

Table 8

Ethnic background : Primary pupils

| Borough | Ethnic category | | | |
|---------|-----------------|---|---|---|
|  | Afro-Caribbean | E.S.W.I | Asian | Others |
| Hammersmith & Fulham | 22.6 | 51.4 | 8.8 | 17.3 |
| Kensington & Chelsea | 13.2 | 42.0 | 6.0 | 38.8 |
| Westminster | 16.9 | 37.6 | 14.6 | 30.9 |
| Camden | 7.9 | 55.3 | 17.1 | 19.7 |
| Islington | 15.2 | 54.3 | 9.4 | 21.1 |
| Hackney | 30.1 | 33.4 | 16.1 | 20.7 |
| Tower Hamlets | 6.8 | 40.6 | 44.6 | 8.0 |
| Greenwich | 5.9 | 78.2 | 7.5 | 8.4 |
| Lewisham | 19.7 | 64.9 | 3.1 | 12.3 |
| Southwark | 23.5 | 57.3 | 4.7 | 14.6 |
| Lambeth | 32.8 | 44.0 | 6.8 | 16.4 |
| Wandsworth | 21.0 | 53.9 | 9.9 | 15.2 |
| Total | 18.5 | 52.7 | 12.4 | 16.4 |

**Table 9**
**Ethnic background : Secondary pupils**

| Borough | Ethnic category | | | |
| | Afro-Caribbean | E.S.W.I | Asian | Others |
| --- | --- | --- | --- | --- |
| Hammersmith & Fulham | 20.1 | 55.4 | 5.0 | 19.5 |
| Kensington & Chelsea | 14.3 | 42.2 | 9.4 | 34.2 |
| Westminster | 18.0 | 47.8 | 13.6 | 20.5 |
| Camden | 8.5 | 63.1 | 8.6 | 19.8 |
| Islington | 15.3 | 50.9 | 11.6 | 22.2 |
| Hackney | 24.3 | 38.5 | 18.6 | 18.6 |
| Tower Hamlets | 9.2 | 43.7 | 39.0 | 8.1 |
| Greenwich | 6.6 | 82.6 | 5.7 | 5.2 |
| Lewisham | 21.6 | 69.4 | 2.9 | 10.5 |
| Southwark | 21.6 | 60.2 | 3.6 | 14.6 |
| Lambeth | 30.8 | 43.3 | 7.1 | 18.8 |
| Wandsworth | 22.9 | 54.6 | 10.2 | 12.3 |
| Total | 17.2 | 56.7 | 11.0 | 15.1 |

# 8 A view of London life

*A H Halsey*

There is a British tradition of utopianism with respect, or rather disrespect, of urban life. No doubt this tradition has in some form found its way into New York, but here I am concerned to underline its influence on the history of thought and action in the planning of London and the attitudes of people to the expected quality of metropolitan life. The tradition is ancient. Ruth Glass remarks it as having preceded the Roman invasion before Christ (Glass 1955). Certainly the British variant of Christian civilisation was adapted to an agrarian way of life over a thousand years, paradoxically defying the association that civicism has borne to civilisation in the evolution of human society. Thus a characteristic strain of anti-urbanism is to be found in the original book of the utopian genre - Thomas More's *Utopia* in 1516.

Sixteenth-century London offered a life of low quality by the standards of the present day. The expectation of life at birth was about 35 years. Infants could be regarded only tentatively as potential adults. Not only mortality but also morbidity was ever present in a world of ill-understood endemic disease, high risks of fire, and precarious food supply. London was a squalid, insanitary mess of crowded hovels. More described it himself in a letter to his old friend John Colet, Dean of St Paul's Cathedral, in 1504. The city according to More was a place of wickedness:

> *No matter where you go, you find feigned love and the honeyed poison of flatterers, and there are always hatred, quarrels and the din of the market. Wherever you turn your eyes, what else will you see but confectioners, fishmongers, butchers, cooks, poulterers, fishermen, fowlers, who supply the materials for gluttony and the world's lord, the devil? Houses block out light and hide us from the heavens.*

By contrast, in the country:

> *wherever you cast your eyes, the smiling face of the earth greets you,*
> *the sweet fresh air invigorates you, the very sight of the heavens*
> *charms you. There you see nothing but the generous gifts of nature*
> *and the traces of our primeval innocence.* (Marius 1984: 3)

One way of interpreting More's *Utopia* is as a vision of London reformed in
the exuberant spirit of a renaissance social engineer.    More's 45,000
Londoners had had their welfare organisation in relief of the poor and their
hospital provision plundered by rural greed. The capital of Utopia, Amaurot,
was a glorious reformation.  A piped water supply, wide streets in front and
delightful gardens behind three-storey houses with flat roofs and glass
windows, all owned in common and democratically governed.  Four great
hospitals served the city, clean and devotedly staffed. There was a guaranteed
provision to the young, the old, the healthy and the sick, of adequate food,
clothing, shelter, and nursing.  Nor was it an entirely fanciful escapism.  The
supply and control of material amenities was ensured by directed labour,
ascetic clothing, cultural unfreedom, and anti-individualism, in a pattern which
could be summarised as an idealised version of the kind of communist state
that has recently been in full retreat from the human stage.

   The terms in which More discussed the quality of urban life have never
subsequently disappeared from the British literature.    Given that the
underlying expectation is one of universalising high standards of amenity, it
can even be said that the two vivid sketches of London with which Howard
Davies begins his introductory overview of the conference are descended from
the same tradition (**Chapter 1**).  He sits apolitically on the fence but leans
rather towards optimism. If we now glance at the view of London entertained
by James Boswell and Dr Samuel Johnson in the eighteenth century we are
reminded of Davies's first caricature of the privileged classes.

   Johnson's hackneyed eulogy is sometimes quoted in dismissal of the
anti-urban tradition: in fact it is a minority opinion of the privileged which
can be put into perspective by Frederick Pottle's introduction to Boswell's
*London Journal, 1762-73* (Pottle 1950).  Pottle reminds us that the journey
from Edinburgh to London by stage-coach or post-chaise took four days.  In
London itself you travelled on foot, by hackney-coach or by sedan chair - a
single seated vehicle carried on poles by two men.  There were few or no
hotels in London in 1762.  Visitors who were not put up by relatives or
friends went to an inn and then looked about for private lodgings.

> *Downing Street, where Boswell lodged during the greater part of his*
> *stay in London, is near St James Park, and in the park Boswell*
> *obtained much of his amusement. There he could see the Footguards*
> *being drilled and paraded; and there, in the Mall, he could stroll back*
> *and forth in the company of ladies of the Court. After sundown the*
> *Park was given over to ladies of another kind, and being unlighted*
> *and unguarded except for an occasional raid from the police office in*

> *Bow Street, it was the scene of a good deal of business in a wicked*
> *way. The gates were locked at ten at night, but sixty-five hundred*
> *people had keys issued by authority, and nobody knows how many*
> *unauthorised keys were in use. The twentieth-century reader will*
> *perhaps be not too much surprised by the record of Boswell's traffic*
> *al fresco with ladies of the town in the Park, since he may have heard*
> *that such things occasionally happen today ...* (Pottle 1950: 25-6)

Pottle was writing in the innocence of 1950 and perhaps had not himself
heard of the customs obtaining in the Bois de Boulogne in Paris:

> *but he may well be astonished by what appears to be the extreme*
> *recklessness on Boswell's part in conducting such transactions in the*
> *streets and on the bridges of the city. If so he must be reminded that*
> *in 1762 few of the streets of London were lighted at all and that most*
> *of the side streets and alleys were dark as the pit. The police force*
> *was of the slenderest. A single watchman, often old and decrepit,*
> *made the rounds with a lantern crying the hour and giving evil-doers*
> *plenty of warning of his approach. If you wanted light, you hired a*
> *link-boy (boy with a flaring torch of pitch and tow) to precede you.*
> (Pottle 1950: 26)

The river was the great thoroughfare and in the daytime the leisured classes
would hire a rowboat with a uniformed waterman to take them up and down,
perhaps to visit the pleasure grounds and gardens at Kensington, Ranelagh in
Chelsea, or Vauxhall on the Surrey side. Young men loose on the town
would spend a good deal of time in coffee houses (where newspapers were
liberally supplied) or in chop-houses or taverns or at one of the three theatres
(the Royal Opera House, Drury Lane and Covent Garden). Consumer
sovereignty had a stronger meaning in those days. According to Pottle, the
theatres:

> *opened at four and the plays began at six. One could not secure a*
> *seat in the pit or galleries except by occupying it or by sending a*
> *servant to occupy it. In 1762 nobody could be made to stand in*
> *queues; consequently there was always a dreadful jam at the entrances*
> *and people were often seriously hurt trying to get in ... The right of*
> *theatre-goers to make an uproar if they disliked a piece was legally*
> *established and freely exercised ... To give the actors some protection*
> *from theatre mobs, a row of sharp spikes was set up along the front*
> *of the stage. 'Sitting at the spikes' was the eighteenth-century way of*
> *saying that one had a front seat in the orchestral stalls.*
> (Pottle 1950: 25)

So much for Howard Davies' first sketch, transposed to the eighteenth
century. But much of the nineteenth-century literature was concentrated on
an elaboration of the second sketch - the threatening underclass confronted by

social control.    There are several versions of different political stripes.
Charles Dickens' is perhaps the most famous.  The mob, whether in London
or Paris, is nowhere more awesomely portrayed, and his depiction (in
*Barnaby Rudge*, 1841) of the 1780 Gordon riots remains a classic.  But the
destitute as distinct from the lumpenproletariat have also been the object of
copious description.    Here again Dickens is probably the outstanding
chronicler of classical urban industrial slums.  In *Bleak House*, for example
he offers graphic contrast between the country estate of Sir Leicester
Deadlock and the East End quarter inhabited by Jo, the illiterate
crossing-sweeper.  This literature is not, however, by any means all fiction.
There are propaganda pamphlets like Mearns' *Bitter Cry of Outcast London*
(1883) and eventually the much more disciplined and reliable social survey
productions by Charles Booth (1891-1903) and Beatrice Webb (1926) which
have the merit of crucially softening if not destroying the dichotomy of
warring classes fostered by Marxists and substituting a more complex and
accurate kaleidoscope of varied urban conditions, including what is most
important, the skilled and respectable London workman and his family who
has constituted the backbone of metropolitan society, despite all attempts to
write him out of history.   The decent working class and the consistently
neglected lower middle class clerks and shop assistants, living spatially and
familiarly restricted lives within the "Great Wen" (Cobbett's phrase), are in
fact the bulk of Londoners at least since the beginning of industrialism.
Moreover the lesser professionals and junior managers have played an
essential part in blurring the edges of contrast between poverty and opulence.
Richard Church's autobiography, *Over the Bridge*, while bringing out the
immensity of the social distance travelled by those who cross Battersea Bridge
northwards to Chelsea, also gives us a poignant account of the precariously
intermediate social status of the families of the lowest echelons of the civil
service and the school teachers in the first decade of the twentieth century
(Church 1955).
    Marx and Engels were, of course, remorseless dichotomisers.    But
interestingly Engels is concerned to point to something still more fundamental
to the understanding of the quality of urban life in the industrial age - the
triumph of individualism.  Here is Engels' view of London in 1844:

> *A town such as London, where a man may wander for hours together*
> *without reaching the beginning of the end, without meeting the*
> *slightest hint which could lead to the inference that there is open*
> *country within reach, is a strange thing.  This colossal centralisation,*
> *this heaping together of two and a half millions of human beings at*
> *one point, has multiplied the power of this two and a half millions a*
> *hundredfold; has raised London to the commercial capital world,*
> *created the giant docks and assembled the thousand vessels that*
> *continually cover the Thames.  I know nothing more imposing than the*
> *view which the Thames offers during the ascent from the sea to*
> *London Bridge.  The masses of buildings, the wharves on both sides,*
> *especially from Woolwich upwards, the countless ships along both*

*shores, crowding ever closer and closer together, until, at last, only a narrow passage remains in the middle of the river, a passage through which hundreds of steamers shoot by one another; all this is so vast, so impressive, that a man cannot collect himself, but is lost in the marvel of England's greatness before he sets foot upon English soil.*

*But the sacrifices which all this has cost became apparent later. After roaming the streets of the capital a day or two, making headway with difficulty through the human turmoil and the endless lines of vehicles, after visiting the slums of the metropolis, one realises for the first time that these Londoners have been forced to sacrifice the best qualities of their human nature, to bring to pass all the marvels of civilisation which crowd their city; that a hundred powers which slumbered within them have remained inactive, have been suppressed in order that a few might be developed more fully and multiply through union with those of others. The very turmoil of the streets has something repulsive, something against which human nature rebels. The hundreds of thousands of all classes and ranks crowding past each other, are they not all human beings with the same qualities and powers, and with the same interest in being happy? And have they not, in the end, to seek happiness in the same way, by the same means? And still they crowd by one another as though they had nothing in common, nothing to do with one another, and their only agreement is the tacit one, that each keep to his own side of the pavement, so as not to delay the opposing streams of the crowd, while it occurs to no man to honour another with so much as a glance. The brutal indifference, the unfeeling isolation of each in his private interest become the more repellent and offensive, the more these individuals are crowded together, within a limited space. And, however much one may be aware that this isolation of the individual, this narrow self-seeking, is the fundamental principle of our society everywhere, it is nowhere so shamelessly barefaced, so self-conscious as just here in the crowding of the great city. The dissolution of mankind into monads, of which each one has a separate principle and a separate purpose, the world of atoms, is here carried out to its utmost extreme.*

*Everywhere barbarous indifference, hard egotism on one hand, and nameless misery on the other, everywhere social warfare, every man's house in a state of siege, everywhere reciprocal plundering under the protection of the law, and all so shameless, so openly avowed that one shrinks before the consequences of our social state as they manifest themselves here undisguised, and can only wonder that the whole crazy fabric still hangs together.* (Marx and Engels 1953: 56-7)

**Four themes**

I travelled through England ten years ago (1982) asking myself how half a century of memories could be compressed out of chaos into order. Slowly, as I moved through London and the provinces my confused recollections ordered themselves into four themes. Re-reading my broadcasts at that time, I again see the four themes as relevant to a seminar on the quality of London life today (Halsey 1983). So I reproduce extracts from them so as to illustrate the seminar papers on transport, housing, education and crime, and especially Ken Young's insightful remarks on civility and public space (**Chapter 3**).

The first theme is an age-old tension between urban and rural life. My biography has caricatured the contrast. I grew up among the dirty brick, the smoky streets, little men in baggy trousers, and shapeless women with shopping baskets that made up Kentish Town in the early 1920s. Then I was transported to Liddington in Rutland. A railway journey from the grandiose grime of gothic St Pancras through the more domestic Victorian elegance of Kettering Station in Northamptonshire, with its neat platforms and its decorated iron stanchions, ended finally with a horse and cart across the Welland Valley into an incredible world of rural, medieval sleepiness and loveliness. Stone and thatch, huge skies, vast woods, and unending open fields were my first memories of the English country.

Yet my mother never reconciled herself to what she contemptuously dismissed as "all them sticks" and longed to return to the busy hugger-mugger of the city streets. When I first read the *Communist Manifesto* of 1848 the phrase which leapt out of that strident pamphlet of vulgarised Marxism was "the idiocy of rural life". Marx gave historical credit to the bourgeoisie for our escape from rural stagnation. I had to give the credit to the London Midland and Scottish railway, which gave railway servants periodic free passes to go anywhere in the country. We always went back to St Pancras.

The tension never ceased, and I came to accept it as not only a private experience but as an integral part of the national psyche. In the end it gave me two patriotisms, the one of the soil, the other of the Cenotaph. Occasionally they would come together when we would gather mushrooms from the fields and send them along the track to far off St Pancras to line our pockets with heavy coins and fill the stomachs of the metropolitans.

Early one summer morning in 1941 my father came from the signal box off the night shift and knocked me up. We went across the fields with our baskets. "Well, lad", he said, "the war's as good as over bar the shouting. They've invaded Russia: it's the same mistake as last time". My feelings were mixed. I was waiting to go into the Air Force, and my juvenile bravado insisted that we could beat the Germans ourselves as our fathers had. At the same time there was relief and reluctant acknowledgement that we could never win without the Russians and/or the Americans. And under the mixture was the uneasy guilty recognition that I didn't care about our Allies except as instruments to English victory. It was a parochial nation.

The second theme was a kaleidoscope in memory of enormous variation of colour, sound, and smell. England is a Jacob's coat of a country. The black splendour of Liverpool Town Hall, white hawthorn everywhere in the spring, the red mud of Devon, the golden stone of villages scattered from Banbury to Peterborough, and the innumerable greens encircling and shrouding all human settlements from the pale fresh lime trees to the dark gloom of the yew.

The ear of the traveller too is assailed by a great variety of sound if only from what is called common speech. Shaw's *Pygmalion* is not a caricature. A man from Sunderland has only to say "Good morning" to distinguish his origins from the Newcastle man 12 miles away. I remember the two languages which I learned in order to survive the day in a grammar school and the evening in the village street. Scents also linger persistently and pervade my recollection. Coal fires, crushed grass, road tarmac and pig styes are vivid olfactory English memory. I can still smell the foetid clammy stink of urine and stale vegetables in the kitchens at the wrong end of the street by contrast with the carbolic soap and boot polish of the respectable families.

Then, third, there was the hierarchy. A sociologist may refine it into abstractions, but no-one could grow up in England without acquiring a deep personal-cum-anthropological knowledge of class and status. This is the England to which I look back in unforgiving anger. Two memories must suffice to evoke it. On one occasion in the 'thirties the tram from Kentish Town was slow. My mother, the latest baby, my sister, my brother, and I rushed into the vault of St Pancras Station and bundled with our impedimenta into the corridor of a first-class carriage seconds before the train drew out. A large, florid-faced man in a pinstripe suit flung open the compartment door to demand of my mother whether she had a first-class ticket. A few years later I was youth hostelling through Bath and idling beside the entrance to a hotel in one of those stately crescents of classical eighteenth-century architecture when I heard the female version of the same baying and arrogant voice asking at the reception desk to be served with coffee. A mumbling apologetic but stubborn west-country voice replied that the kitchens were closed; and the lady stormed out with the parting judgement of the authentic English metropolitan snob "these damned provinces".

Fourth, and finally, there is the sense of tension between change and changelessness in English society. The London townscape has been transformed in my lifetime - invaded, that is, by the international architecture of Corbusier and modern brutalism. New towns appear and old industrial development falls into decay. But underneath lies the never-defeated countryside, and English sentiment refuses to give up its rural nostalgia. The Victorian hierarchy has virtually collapsed and two generations of 'class abatement' have changed poverty from the common experience of the working class into the misfortunes of the old, the sick, the homeless, the unemployed and the locally blighted. Yet the House of Lords, the public schools, the phoney farms of the millionaires, and the shabby back streets of Toxteth or Brixton are still with us. I feared that my island journeys would confirm a strident new impulse of destructiveness as a result of the frenzied search of a new government for a new private enterprise and governmental detachment. Nevertheless, my expectation was that the hope of progress could not have disappeared. Certainly it is a fundamental element in the experience of my generation. We still believe in the possibility of the new Jerusalem. For me it is bound up with escape from parochialism and provincialism. I remember Amy Johnson landing in her Moth on the expansive lawns of the local lord and experiencing the childish vision of a larger world of opportunity out there. I flew my first Tiger Moth in 1942 over a wintry Wiltshire and felt again the exhilaration of movement in a flimsy vehicle surrounded by towering cumulus clouds and the English panorama below. England is different. As Orwell wrote "When you come back to England from any foreign country, you have immediately the sensation of breathing a different air" (Orwell 1950: 75). The difference for me is the possibility of new freedom and new justice built on ancient solidarity.

1984 was emerging from the worst winter for 20 years into a bright new spring. Easter came, and I set out on a series of excursions through England and Scotland to record impressions of my country and my compatriots.

It so happened, the night before my departure, that my family had been arguing long and passionately about patriotism. The idea divides the generations. My generation distinguishes between nationalism and patriotism, feeling both, but with guilt for the first and pride in the second. How could it be otherwise? My father's tin hat from the trenches of the First World War hung behind the pantry door as a symbol of courage and sacrifice. We were ordinary Labour people who never for a moment believed with the Communists that 'the working man has no country'. "But what does your country mean?", my children asked. "Is it Kentish Town where you were born, the borders of Rutland where you grew up, or north Oxford where you live now? Does it include Ireland where your grandmother was born? Are you not a European? Do you not have more in common with American social scientists than with the railway drivers and the signalmen in your own country?"

As to nationalism and patriotism, they argued, that is a distinction without a difference. War and looting and killing have been justified with semantic ease under either term, and we must abandon both if the human race is to survive.

I listened to all this, or at any rate to its underlying moral sentiments, with respect. The Falklands war was just beginning and gave sharp focus to the argument. It strikes me as characteristic of modern idealism that the primordial ties of individual people to life - I mean family, locality, race, religion, and nation - are seen much more readily as barriers to virtue rather than vehicles of it. The historical, paradoxical and awkward complication is that they are both; and stubbornly persistent in their nurturing of both conflict and accord. Heroism and tenderness are found in family and community. But love of country and pride of race have also killed millions in our own life time. The whole cast of the modern liberal mind is towards evading the paradox and regarding these primordial bonds as the vestigial inheritance of past barbarism which will either be discarded by a progressive future or will destroy us all. The optimistic version of this theory of history seems to be strongly entrenched in the conventional wisdom offered by teachers to children.

By contrast, the village classroom that I remember from the 'twenties was steeped in officially-sanctioned nationalism. The world map was red for the Empire and dull brown for the rest, with Australia and Canada vastly exaggerated in size by Mercator's projection. The Greenwich meridian placed London at the centre of the world. Empire Day and November 11th ritualised an established national supremacy. What my children underestimate is the degree to which the teaching of the history of the *Malvinas* in Argentine schools is of a piece with less than ancient British practice. What perhaps I underestimate is the impact of Hiroshima on the outlook of the post-war European generations.

Nevertheless, I knew that neither patriotism nor nationalism had been abolished by my children's ethical affirmations. The previous September, a Gallup poll had asked people throughout western Europe about their attitudes to their country. The question put was: "Of course we all hope that there will not be another war, but if it were to come to that, would you be willing to fight for your country?" (Abrams *et al* 1985: 160-61). The British sample was distinctively the most positive: nearly two-thirds declared themselves unequivocally willing to fight for their country, compared with only a quarter of the Belgians and the Italians. For good or ill, a sense of national belonging and obligation is, and remains, a serious fact of the British life which I was intending to explore.

My chosen method was to be a self-conscious traveller. I would check the evidence from impersonal surveys and from intimate family conversations by something in-between - encounters with people on my journeys. I boarded a bus in north Oxford on the first morning, keen to know what sort of people would fill the in-between and so inform me about the meaning of words like patriotism, nationalism, and country. Two women got on at the next stop. They both wore smart flowered frocks, with the neatly cosmetic face to match that one associates with the devotees of *Come Dancing*. Whether or not they were representative compatriots they were, like millions of others, discussing the Falklands crisis. One of them suddenly challenged the other to remember an old song:

> *You'll find your life will begin*
> *The very moment you're in ARGENTINA.*

"Fancy that", she said, "And now some of our best people are going there."

It didn't matter that the rest of the conversation receded from me on to the pavement. The point was that I was on the way to London and thence through the chaotic and fragmented network of human exchanges which make up a national life. Yet the tradition also makes the traveller unusual - an outsider or marginal man moving through a static and parochial people. So Henry Mayhew records in the 1840s, that he talked to Cockneys who had never seen the sea and had the vaguest conception of the whereabouts of

Southend (Mayhew (1861) 1981).  And historians tell us that 95 percent of eighteenth-century Frenchmen were born and buried in the same *département*.

Mobility is now, of course, common experience.  People migrate and communicate, scattering families, inter-marrying races, mingling religions, and obscuring national boundaries.  Indeed, this first morning itself illustrated how far and how fast the world can become a village.  For I had talked on the telephone to a colleague in New York, posted a letter to New Zealand, read news from Buenos Aires, and travelled from Oxford to Paddington and into the City by 9 am.  Present mobility involves a world-wide connection of people and places.  Distance is obliterated by modern transport and telephone.  But that is not all.  Travelling also, especially in England, always gives me the sense of movement through time as well as through space.  For me the train from Oxford to London is also a time machine into the past.  My great-grandfather had made his way into the metropolis by a very different mode of transport, on foot with pick and shovel, as a navvy 100 years ago.

My train drew into the platform.  The carriages had been brought out of a siding somewhere, perfunctorily hosed and cleaned for a journey in a way which couldn't disguise their grubbiness.  The blue and green check of the upholstery of the 1960s and 1970s was soiled, and the windows speckled with dirt darkening a dark morning.  I imagine that the uniforms of the porters, guards, and ticket collectors were inspired by some kind of exotic impulse of gaiety 20 years before.  The caps in particular, with their turned-up edges and red or gold ribbon trim, look French, but the functionaries insist on wearing them straight over their knobbly English faces, and so restore the appearance of drab British solemnity.  They are anything but 'nonchalant'.  Inherited custom and practice modify and absorb novelty.  Change comes surreptitiously or else is merely added to traditional routine.  So it is with journeys.

The whole of the history of travel technology, which runs from the pedestrian to the space rocket, is still with us.  Even in my own memory, for example, a thousand pictures of people moving come back from time and across space.  The images crowd together: running across a Northamptonshire field in 1934 to carry the news of the cricket score wafted by wireless waves to a crystal set from Sydney in Australia; the railway station at Mafeking in 1944, watching an African child riding backward pillion on his mother's back along a footpath parallel with the track; California in 1956 alongside a huge steam engine of the Southern Pacific Railway looking like a huge romantic dinosaur by comparison with the gleaming and fragile Dodge 1951 which I was driving on the highway towards San Francisco; Tokyo 1966 and the impenetrable chatter of a Japanese wedding party seeing its newly married couple on to the electric train which rushes along to Kyoto at 120 miles an hour.  And there are still in my memory the more or less extinct forms of transport which are trams and prams and horses and carts, and the go-karts which boys would put together from orange boxes and old pram wheels before the plastic age.

My journeys now would challenge me to make sense of the past in the present.  The capital was the obvious place to begin.  From Paddington I made my way immediately to the heart and origin of Britain.

The City of London on that first morning renewed my consciousness of connection. It was already awake, alive with people, buildings going up and coming down, messages on placards, vehicles and entrances from all the centuries and all parts of the world. The most obvious messages were about financial connections. The banks of Minneapolis, Wells Fargo, and Kuwait, and the Halifax Building Society are abstract symbols of money and trade with men in sombre suits and women in smart summer clothes, the men carrying black attaché cases, and the women handbags, scurrying obscurely between them, beginning the daily round. A bearded Italian in a navy blue apron with white stripes serves them with coffee and take-away lunches from the modernised interior of an ancient English building, and street names like Coal Lane, Bull Wharf, or Threadneedle Street remind me that morning in the streets of abstract symbols has its continuities with previous ages of more direct and concrete human relations. And the Italian greets his regular customers with a familiarity which informs the casual visitor that there exists a network of human contact below the surface of impersonal and anonymous trading. For me, the *entrée* as a stranger has to be a cash transaction. But even that can quickly dissolve into the human reciprocities of passing the time of day. Human beings refuse to confine themselves to the cash nexus. The social always tends to overcome the economic relation.

London for me is spatially ambiguous. Of course it is the metropolis but England, its country, is essentially provincial. The City of London is still more ambiguous. The normal notion of Britain is of westernness. But the City is on the east side of London, the Thames flows towards the Orient, the warehouses of the dockside import tea from Assam, and Liverpool Street Station is the beginning of the Great Eastern Railway. Liverpool Street is not one of the famous London exits. For those I must take the tube west and north round the Circle line. But before I went I paused by the ticket office to look at a huge marble wall plaque listing the names of railway servants who fell in the First World War. Again I was travelling in time. All the familiar English names - the Clarks, the Coopers, and the Smiths - a roll-call recalling their vocational origins in a pre-industrial division of labour. It is another country now. The chandlers, the wheelwrights, the saddlers and the ostlers must be obscure trades and professions to today's children, even those who still bear their names.

Victorian modernity and urbanism stand between the old and the new world; acres and acres of assertive brickwork. Yet the older agrarian order is never quite defeated, and greenery in the English summer appears perennially in its remorseless counter-attack, trying to engulf the brickwork, to recapture its ancient territory. Rural nostalgia and anti-urbanism are a persistent motif of the English - perhaps because we were the first industrial nation. You see it expressed everywhere in the preference for low density, low-rise housing and gardens. On the tube the advertisement read "You get home quicker with a Return ticket". And home is depicted as a seventeenth-century scene - a return to Sylvania, chickens, and a Brueghel-like figure playing a harp.

If anything stands unassailable above the battle it is St Pancras Station. It belongs to my earliest memories. I was born in Kentish Town: and to my infant eye St Pancras was a mile high.  Built for ever, the last great Gothic cathedral (albeit secular), towering arches and pinnacles reaching to a technological heaven; shining steel and glass canopy emulating the Crystal Palace; elaborate oak panelling in the booking office rivalling the dignity of the Treasury.  In short, an enormous monument to all eternity.

Yet entering it now I saw the contradiction.  Eternity is calm and still, but the ephemeral is just as much part of the travelling scene.  The paper cup and the discarded newspaper on the tables in the buffet, the notice boards with a laminate coating hiding a flimsy chipboard, and the electronic indicators which flash train times and platform numbers momentarily before obliterating them, also for ever.  But not my memories.  Time may be, as the Remembrance Day hymn insists, "Like an ever rolling stream".  But the subjective time of my recollections and anticipations remains free to transport me to a when and a where of my own choosing.

Nevertheless objective time is inexorable.  So from another point of view it is a good first definition of us all that we are slaves to the watch, the clock, the diary and the calendar.  Subjective time releases the human imagination.  But without the idea of objective time, the spectacular achievements of science which depend so heavily on the accurate recording of sequence and duration would not have been possible.  The clocks would not control the trains, I could not the beat the bounds of my country in the excursions of a short summer, and the American Secretary of State could not travel across time zones, jet lag or no jet lag, to synchronise the prevention or acceleration of war between countries 8,000 miles apart.

## Another Easter Monday

The number of public holidays is said to be a rough inverse index of a nation's puritanism.  On that scale Britain is nearer to Communism than to Roman Catholic Christianity.  For Brazil has 18 public holidays, Bulgaria has five and we have six.  So it was that on Easter Monday I set out to seek my birthplace - Kentish Town.

It was exactly nine in the morning when I descended the steep stone steps out of St Pancras Station, and turned north.  I still half expected to catch the tram to Prince Albert Street and up towards Parliament Hill Fields.  The street between St Pancras and King's Cross struck me as less grim and grimy than it was in the 1930s, and yet also much more littered and untidy.  The tram tickets have gone, but so has the cheap labour of the dustman and the street sweeper.  Their greater affluence and fewer numbers give victory to the modern litter of plastic and cellophane.  As I walked northwards Camden Borough Council assaulted my eyes with hoardings boasting of its rapid house building.

It was true that new tenements and squares in dirty London brick had replaced some of the old Victorian and Edwardian terraces.  It was true, too, that there were very few ancient buildings except for the old St Pancras parish church.  But the late Victorian burst of railway energy still dominated the landscape with its black arches, its monumentally substantial pubs, schools and hospitals, and its atmosphere of brick on brick for ever, occasionally relieved by decorative ironwork.

Kentish Town was still for the most part asleep. Those who were abroad seemed to be people cut off from the cellular domestic life of houses and flats, either permanently because they were old men on the tramp, or temporarily because they had business with dogs or cars or health which had taken them into the street to walk or jog or earnestly to inspect the inside of a raised car bonnet. The invisible majority, I assumed, were preparing in a leisurely way for the bank holiday. The visible minority had in common that they were not *formally* working, however busy they were, and even the few men I noticed on ladder or scaffold here and there were devotees of what we now call the informal economy. Nearly all the shops were closed and barred except for one or two newsagents. I turned into a workman's café on Camden High Street and sat over thick stale tea of the traditional brew to eavesdrop on the conversation of those displaced from the domesticities. They were all male, including the Polish Cockney proprietor. Two retired long-distance lorry drivers carried on a desultory argument in guttural Glaswegian dialect, about the best route to Guildford. An old tramp sat in the corner muttering obscenities to himself in west country tones which rose and fell like the tide on some dimly remembered Devon coast. Two younger men were local Cockneys exchanging rapid diphthongs and lazy consonants - that is, the familiar fast and lively talk which was my own mother tongue. They intended to try and finish putting in a new bath in a nearby house before going up to Highbury to the football game - Arsenal *versus* Tottenham Hotspur.

The match was also my destination, otherwise I would have been tempted to give up the day as pointless for the traveller since by common consent the normal life of the office and factory was formally suspended, and domestic life is by definition private. I was the man in the street, and therefore temporarily dispossessed.

I felt this most acutely as I turned off Highgate Road into College Lane where my parents in 1922 took two rooms in one of the eighteenth-century cottages which have survived urbanisation, expansion, slumdom and gentrification, through to the present day. The lane was as I remembered it except that part of the old wall had disappeared to reveal a post-war school and a housing estate. *The Fields Beneath* is Gillian Tindall's title for a diary of Kentish Town (1980). My ancestors, too, I would add, are buried *there* as well as in my memory of a grey, smoky, crowded place of hundreds of uncles and aunts. My father was one of 18 (all baptised in the parish church) and my mother one of 12, and the tribe ramified all the way from Camden Town and the shunting yards up to Parliament Hill Fields and across to Belsize Park. My grandmother's tenement at the *wrong* end of Upper Park Road has been knocked down, leaving the whole area to the now servantless gentry.

It *was* the wrong end in inter-war days because it housed the servants of the grand Hampstead houses. Kentish Town was much more emphatically not Hampstead then than it is now. So much so that it always seemed wrong and vaguely fraudulent to take the tube to Belsize Park instead of catching the tram to Prince of Wales Road. One would then have to walk down Haverstock Hill past posh people in white stucco mansions and then eastwards abruptly into the unglittering plebeian quarter of tenements and rented rooms.

The social divisions are less crude and simple now. Yet nothing really changes and the fields still lie beneath. Kentish Town has always been a bridge and a battlefield for different ways of life: town and country, house and factory, villa and apartment block, landlord and tenant.

The present lives unheeding in the past. But at one point I fancied I saw a reverse glance. There was a large pub sign over the maroon and buff painted stonework of the *George IV*, depicting Prinny looking down his aristocratic nose with lofty indifference onto the street below. On the pavement stood a West Indian couple: a young woman in a purple pleated skirt, pink jumper and pink head shawl to match, with golden sequins and gold bracelets - a sort of flamingo princess, moving rhythmically from one foot to the other as she told some vivid tale to her stolid, bespectacled boy-friend. Kentish Town has always juxtaposed the incongruous of both the past and the present.

I got on a bus at Pond Street, and went back to King's Cross for the Piccadilly line and the Arsenal. Down the escalator to the bowels of the north London earth - a tube under the *urbs*. I remembered underground travel in the early 'thirties as red, futuristic, H G Wellsian. The tube trains are now rather seedy aluminium by comparison with the BART of the San Francisco Bay area or the Paris *Metro*. My fellow travellers were mostly male adolescents, Highbury-bound. I sensed in them a well-oiled routine. Tough machismo exteriors, faces expressionless, moving or hovering towards hostility, yet not hostile, somehow keeping up a male front, inelegant, yet apparently strongly held by a shared conception of correct apparel which is jeans and sneakers and anorak - all with broad stripes and dominantly navy blue and red colouring. A small gold knob through one pierced ear is currently fashionable. Few traditional football supporters' favours were to be seen - these seemed to be more for young boys aged 10 or 11, often accompanied by their dads in more sombre versions of the standard adolescent garb. These younger boys had red and white scarves and woollen hats. Some even wore the traditional rosette.

Nobody, it seems, is alone, or almost nobody. They thronged the platform mostly in pairs, especially fathers and sons, girls in their late teens, or young couples. Some pairs, I noticed, are black and white, connected by a common Cockney speech. One pair was Swedish, immediately distinguishable to the ear by their curious speech rhythm, and striking the eye, too, not because of their blond hair, but because their clothes are so much cleaner and more finely tailored.

I moved along the concrete tube exit at Highbury with the crowd, emerging blinking into bright sunlight. Already at noon the streets around the stadium were thronged, again mostly by male adolescents, more now with red and white scarves and other Arsenal totems. Late nineteenth-century houses, small, mean, terraced, and semi-detached, are temporarily given over to selling gaudy mementos of the Gunners in general, and this local Derby match in particular.  At every street corner is a hot dog stall.  In the main shopping street there are cafés every few yards, selling fish and chips to those who prefer to eat them in the traditional *ambulando* fashion between old sheets of *The Mirror* or *The Sun*.

I went into one where the offering was a seat at a clean formica-topped table, busily and efficiently run by an Italian family.  Spaghetti bolognese was available as an alternative to fish and chips or the standard combinations of egg, sausage, bacon, beans and chips.  Tea is a standard accompanying drink, and it is assumed that you will drink it before eating the food, and if you want sugar it is added before serving.  The helpings are handsome, the plates clean, the waitress is unceremonious, and the meal is plonked on to the table hot from the stove somewhere hidden in the back.  And it is cheap.  You can be adequately filled with fish and chips and the almost mandatory tea and buttered bread for less than £2 at 1982 prices.  "Love" is the normal appellation whether in Italian or Cockney or Glaswegian English.  It seems that there are always Scots wherever there is football.

This form of pre-match luncheon is not for the adolescent groups: more for the father-son pairs and the young couples.  The two Swedes whom I had noticed on the tube came in just after me.  I noticed again that they were cleaner than either the food or my average compatriot.

The image of Eddie Hapgood or Alex James came vividly back to my mind, and I enjoyed a brief fantasy of their appearance inside the stadium in the brave red and white shirt, billowing white shorts down almost to the knee, hair firmly parted and slicked down with Brylcreem, cut to short back and sides.  In other words, an image of the pre-war working class fantasy of orderly glamour which punctuated and put into high relief the regular monotony of a humdrum work-a-day world.

Again this memory is of the fantastic linked to the mundane in a tightly ordered, even regimented, but collectively self-regulated culture.  And it was a strictly limited culture of clearly demarcated social rules and spheres: between the sexes (the women stayed at home), between the classes (the working men stood on the terraces), between work and leisure (the latter was brief), and between home and away (the locals went *en masse* and mostly on foot only to home matches).  Now all these boundaries of sex, class, locality, and time are crucially loosened.  That perhaps is why one *expects* disorder at a football match, quite apart from any defining influence from television and the mass media.  For those blessed or cursed with memory, the erosion of distinctions of time, place and station *is* disorder.

But perhaps the children of affluence, of easy travel and modern cosmopolitanism, discern order where their parents see only disorder?  I wondered.

In the tube on the way up to Highbury I had contemplated, just above the green-streaked blond hair of an adolescent devotee of punk, the warning notice: "London Transport will press for maximum penalties for anyone committing an assault on a member of staff.  In some cases this can mean LIFE IMPRISONMENT."  Did this mean that war had been declared between officialdom and a new, marauding adolescent culture which had become, or threatened to become, out of civil control?  Was this why I could count over 100 police in the stadium before 500 spectators had turned up?  I wasn't sure. As I waited in a bright sunshine made cold by a north-east wind from Essex and Siberia, the paradox of localism and a form of world citizenship was continually renewed.  All the symbols and verbal exchanges were intensely local - the Gunners' emblems, the Cockney vocabulary.  But at the same time the loudspeakers blared Frank Sinatra's crooning assertion that "Chicago is my kind o'town", and "Seems it never rains in southern California".  And the adverts round the arena celebrated the multinationals: Japanese cars, American banks, Mediterranean holidays.

The rules of football are now standardised throughout the world, but it is only just beyond living memory when vociferous argument about how the game should be played prevented the possibility of matches between teams from Sheffield and London.  A form of soccer was played in ancient China, but the modern game was essentially invented by local British communities who argued with each other for the better part of the nineteenth century as to which variants of the rules should be nationalised.  Moreover, when nationalisation came, though British football spread itself all over the world as a by-product of imperialism, British nationalism was slow to subject itself to international rules, so that we were the founders but not the champions of the international game.

Nationalism still has a sometimes ugly, sometimes comic, expression in the bowler-hatted union jacks of some groups of spectators, and in the rather half-hearted attempts of some of Arsenal fans to boo the Argentinian, Ricky Villa, who played on the Tottenham side.

As the kick-off drew near, parochial disorder asserted itself in what seemed to be a highly ordered fashion, almost as if it had been many times rehearsed. The basic rule is that the riotous and quasi war-like supporters occupy separate ends behind the goal mouths - in this case the Arsenal mob had the north end, and the Spurs mob had the south end, with the neutral and rather more expensively seated spectators in the stands along the two sides.  Trouble was staged at the north-east corner in the form of competitive attempts from both mobs to take possession of that intermediate territory.  It was a crude ballot between four *dramatis personae*.  Peaceable spectators were the majority and stationary.  Then, second, Spurs intruders came round from the south end, and seemed to flow through the first group like a shoal of fish swimming through weeds towards the dense mass of the red and white.  This third group, the Arsenal mob, started to countercharge only to be met by the fourth group of trained police who cut across between the two and roughly repelled both invasions, carrying off an occasional exemplary captive to be paraded along the touch line and either released with stern warnings into his appropriate position on the north or the south end, or in some cases apparently ejected entirely from the ground.

The man sitting next to me in the stand repeated what also sounded like a ritual outrage.  "Gawd love us, what's the matter with 'em.  It's only a game of football."  I noticed that, within 30 seconds of the kick-off, the invasion and counter invasion ceased, and my peaceable neighbour was screaming abuse at the referee for awarding a foul against what seemed to me to be a clear infringement of the rules of the game.

Incidentally, the Arsenal lost. I cannot remember that they ever did so in the 1930s.


## The Archbishop's Commission

By the mid 1980s there was growing concern in Britain about the quality of life in the inner cities. One remarkable manifestation was the Archbishop of Canterbury's appointment of a commission to enquire into the conditions developing in the 'urban priority areas'. The concern of the Church was with the decline of church attendance  but also with the growing evidence of deteriorating conditions of civility as indicated by indices of social deprivation, physical decay and social disorganisation. It was not an exclusively London problem though districts like Hackney had become notorious for bad housing conditions, Tower Hamlets was a place of increasing homelessness among young people, and Brixton was thought of as a concentration of lawlessness and hostile race relations. At all events the Archbishop was convinced that a full-scale investigation was necessary and the Commission, after two years of visiting and taking evidence produced its report in December 1985 under the title *Faith in the City* (1985). The secular dimensions of the report are highly relevant to the seminar's consideration of the American and British contributions. With some oversimplification it may be said that the American contributors tend to take individualist or market consumer views of the problems of government and administration of housing, education, traffic, crime control and employment in New York. The British on the other hand tend to see London through collective, administration and planning eyes. In this perspective the British Conservative government has been American and the Anglican Church has been the mouthpiece of British socialist tradition. We have here therefore a challenge to reconcile two different (but not necessarily completely opposed) philosophies. The balance of the individual and the social, the public and the private, the untrammelled and the regulated, are of the essence in any appraisal of the quality of urban life.


## Concluding remarks

This essay is, in a way, an introduction. It is however appropriate to repeat my main themes. Perhaps most important is the view that London is really an 'anti-city'. True that in the twentieth century there has been the ascendancy and subsequent demise of the London County Council and the Greater London Council from Herbert Morrison to Ken Livingstone, the last great popular king of County Hall. True too that Samuel Johnson and James Boswell in the eighteenth and David and Ruth Glass in the twentieth century have taken more 'Viennese' views of the possibilities of metropolitan culture.

But the persistent ideological bent has always been towards rural nostalgia. Thomas More, Charles Dickens, William Morris and George Orwell have been its chroniclers and Ebenezer Howard, the author of *Garden Cities of Tomorrow* (1902) along with the Institute of Community Studies directed by Michael Young in Bethnal Green have been its analysts and architects. The characteristic low density development of London suburbia has been its main legatee. Visions of reform have been an idealised conception of rurality as the benchmark of a high quality of life and G K Chesterton's *Napoleon of Notting Hill Gate* has been its political hero (1946, 1904).

The London view is also more complaisant. It is difficult if not impossible for British commentators to imagine a London parallel to the film *New Jack City*. New Yorkers like Daniel Bell or Nathan Glazer write appreciatively of London's capacity to renew faith in the civic idea. Another possible outcome of the seminar is an answer to the question of whether New York or London offers the better prospect of high civility and if so for whom?

## References

Abrams M, Gerard D and Timms N (eds) (1985) *Values and Social Change in Britain*, London: Macmillan.

Archbishop's Commission (1985) *Faith in the City*, London: Church House Publishing (December 1985).

Booth C (1981-1903) *Life and Labour of the People in London*, 17 volumes.

Chesterton G K (1946, 1904) *Napoleon of Notting Hill Gate*, London: Penguin.

Church R (1955) *Over the Bridge*, London: Chatton & Windus.

Glass R (1955) Urban Sociology in Great Britain: A Trend Report, *Current Sociology*, **4**, 4, Paris: UNESCO.

Halsey A H (1983) Another English Journey, *The Listener* (6 January-10 February 1983).

Howard E (1902) *Garden Cities of Tomorrow*, Swan, Sonnenschein & Co.

Marius R (1984) *Thomas More*, London: Dent.

Marx K and Engels F (1953) *Karl Marx and Frederick Engels on Britain*, London: Lawrence & Wishart Ltd.

Mayhew H (1861, 1981) *London Labour and the London Poor*, London: Charles Gribbin.

Mearns A (1883) *Bitter Cry of Outcast London*, London: James Clarke.

Orwell G (1950) The Lion and the Unicorn: Socialism and the English Genius in *The Collected Essays, Journalism and Letters of George Orwell Vol 2, 1940-1943*, London: Penguin.

Pottle F (1950) Introduction, in *Boswell's London Journal, 1762-73*, London: Heinemann.

Tindall G (1980) *The Fields Beneath*, London: Paladin.

Webb B (1926) *My Apprenticeship*, London: Longmans.

# Subject Index

## A

Abrams M *et al* 143
Adult education: *see* Education
Alexander C 63
Anglican Church 151
Archbishop's Commission 151
Association of London Authorities
  (ALA) 77, 79
Audit Commission 7, 8, 93, 102, 103

## B

Beggars, begging 60
Benzeval *et al* 6
Best R *et al* 100
Bianchini F 62
Booth C 138
Borough, London 112-113
Boswell J 136-137
Bourgois P 20
Boyle and Smaje 7
Bramley G 104
British Crime Survey (BCS) 36, 43, 57
British Rail (BR) 3-4, 69, 70-71, 77,
  78, 144
Brownhill S *et al* 95, 102
Buck N H 17
Buck N H *et al* 14, 24, 31, 53
Buck N H and Fainstein N 14
Buck N H and Gordon I R 22
Buses 69, 70, 72-73, 75, 78

## C

Car(s) 53-54, 70, 72
Casual employment 18, 19, 20, 31
Central Statistical Office (CSO) 27, 84,
  86, 92, 96
Channel Tunnel 71, 72
Chartered Institute of Transport 69,
  78-79
Chesterton G K 152
Church R 138
City of London 14, 145
City Technology College 112, 118, 126
Class, Social 138, 141
Cohen R B 15
Coles A 84
Coleman A 56
Commission of Excellence in Education
107-108
Communities and Homes in London/
  Council for the Protection of Rural
  England 85
Commuting 13-14, 25, 69-71
Confederation of British Industry, CBI
  10, 85
Congestion 70-71
Conservative, Conservative Party 5, 9,
  25, 27, 80, 83, 103, 115, 151
Coopers and Lybrand Deloitte 4, 5, 8,
  9, 11
Council of Mortgage Lenders 88, 90,
  92
Council tenancy 17, 24, 30

Crawford A *et al* 40
Crime 7-8
Crime,
    fear of 39-40, 62
    measurement of 35-36, 38
    public concern about 39-40, 42
**Crime in London: an assessment**
    35-45
Crime rates 36-38, 41-42, 45
    *also see* New York
Crook A *et al* 93
Cullen G 47


**D**

Dahrendorf, Sir Ralf 2-3
Davies, H 136, 137
Decentralisation,
    of employment 21, 31, 53
    of population 21, 52-53, 94, 98
    of retailing 54
Deindustrialisation 14, 15, 18, 20,
    21-22
Department of Environment 83-84, 86,
    87, 89, 94, 100, 102
Department of Transport 77-78
Dickens, Charles 138, 152
van Dijk J and Mayhew P 43
van Dijk J *et al* 43
Disorder, public 39
Docklands 32, 72, 99, 101, 102
    *also see* London Docklands
        Development Corporation
Docklands Forum and Birkbeck
    College (DFBC) 27, 28
Docklands Light Railway 69, 75, 79
Douglas, Porteous J 56
Duster T 18-19, 20-21


**E**

East London Compact 28
Education 4-5, 27, 28, 31, 107-133
    adult 122
    higher 121-122
    nursery 116-117
    special 122-123
Education policy 110-111, 112-115,
    125, 126-128
        *also see* Education
Education Reform Act 1988 5, 114
Elias N 62
**Employment issues** 13-34
Engels F 138-139

Enterprise zones 32
Equal opportunities 27, 28, 119
Ermish J 85
Ethnic inequality 29-30
    and education 119-120
Ethnic minorities 16, 17, 123


**F**

Fainstein S S *et al* 14, 15
Female employment 16
Fischer C S 63
Football 147, 148-151
Fothergill S and Gudgin G 14
Friedmann J and Wolff G 15


**G**

General practitioners, GPs 6
Girouard M 52
Glass R 135, 152
Gordon I R 4-5, 6, 17, 21, 24, 25, 26
Grace G 110
Greater London Council (GLC) 2,
    9-10, 25-26, 28, 30, 73, 74, 75 79,
        80, 98, 151
Greater London Enterprise Board
    (GLEB) 26-27
Greater London Living Standards
    Survey 17-18, 32
Greve J 93
Gurr T R *et al* 20


**H**

Hall E T 63
Hall P G 31
Halsey A H 140
Hamilton P 62
Healthcare 6-7
Health authorities 6-7
Heath A 29
Heseltine, Rt Hon M 2-3, 10
Higher education: *see* Education
Hillier Parker 10
Hills J 91
Homeless, homelessness 9, 85-86, 92,
    93-94, 98, 102, 103
Hope T and Hough M 57, 62
Hospitals 6, 7
Hough M and Mayhew P 7-8, 43
House prices 88-94, 100
Household size 87

**Housing** 83-106
Housing 8-9, 16, 31, 83-106
Housing associations 9, 86, 89-90, 91,
    92, 94-97, 98-99, 101, 102
Housing estates 56, 94, 103
Housing policy 83-84, 85, 90-93, 95,
    97-98, 99, 100, 101-103
        *also see* Housing
Howard E 152


**I**

Incivility 57
Income distribution 17
Inner London Education Authority
    (ILEA) 28, 108-109, 110, 112,
    113-114, 115, 116, 122
Institute of Metropolitan Studies 4
Institution of Civil Engineers 77
International Crime Survey (ICS) 36,
    37-38, 43
Isle of Dogs Enterprise Zone 27


**J**

Jackson A 53, 63
Jacobs J 56
James H 63
Job creation 25-26, 27
Job saving 26-27
Johnson, Dr Samuel 136
Jones G S 20,21
Jones T *et al* 36


**K**

Kentish Town 140, 141, 142, 146,
    147-148
King A D 14
Kleinman M P 92, 95
Kleinman M P and Whitehead C M E
    92


**L**

Labour, Labour Party 9, 25, 28, 31-32,
    80, 115, 142
Landry C and Worpole K 48, 54
Layard R *et al* 24
Levi-Strauss C 60
Levitas G 52, 55
Liberal Democrats 9
Lively P 62

Local authorities 25, 26, 28
    and education 111, 114-115, 120
    and housing 100-101, 102-103
    *also see* Education; Housing; Local
        government
Local authority housing: *see* Housing
Local government 5, 7, 9-10, 72-73,
    80, 115, 116
        and education 110, 114
        and housing 97-98, 101
        *also see* Education; Housing;
            Local Authorities; Local
            government
Local Government Commission 7
Local Management of Schools 111, 116
Lofland L H 49, 50-51, 56, 60, 62
London Borough of Newham 36
London Boroughs' Association 9, 77, 79
London Docklands Development
    Corporation (LDDC) 25, 27
*London Labour Plan* 25-26
London/New York survey, crime-related
    issues 42-43
London Planning Advisory Committee
    (LPAC) 4, 76-77, 79-80, 85, 91, 98,
    100, 103
London Regional Liberal Democrats 9
London Research Centre 88, 91, 94,
    102
London Research Centre/Association
    of London Authorities 85
London and South-East Regional
    Planning Conference 77, 96
London Transport 4, 73, 75
London Transportation Study 73-74, 75
London Underground 4, 68-69, 70-73,
    74-76, 77, 78, 148
Lynch K 62


**M**

McAuley I 62
McGahey R M 31
Maclennan D and Williams R 83
Manufacturing, manufacturing industry
    14, 15, 21-22
Marins R 135-136
Marx, Marxism 138, 140
Marx K and Engels 138-139
Masterman C F G 53
Mawson J and Miller D 27, 31-32
Maxwell, Robert 6, 7
Mayhew H 143-144
Mayhew P and Aye Maung N 43
Mayor 2-3, 9, 10, 80

Meadows *et al* 22,23
Mearns A 138
Mesospace 56
Milgram S 59, 60-61
More, Thomas 135-136, 152
Mortimore P 109-110, 114
Motorcar: *see* Car(s)
Mumford L 63
Murray K and Willie D 49


N


Naismith, D 5, 107-133
National Curriculum 111, 116, 117,
120,  125, 127
National Federation of Housing
   Associations 95, 98
Neighbourhoods 56-57
Network South East: *see* British Rail
New York 2, 4, 8, 9, 15, 16, 21, 29,
   30, 31, 68, 69, 151, 152
      crime rates in 37, 38, 41-42
Newman O 56
Newman P 50, 53
Nursery Education: *see* Education


O


OECD 63
Olympics 3, 10
Orwell G 142, 152
Out-migration: *see* Decentralisation
Owner-occupation: *see* Housing


P


Painter K *et al* 36
Parks, public 52
Parks R 58, 61
'Parochial realm' 50, 56
Part-time employment 16
Pedestrianisation 63
Planning 8, 30-31, 61-62, 96, 98,
   100-101, 102
      *see also* Transport planning
Police 8
   public attitudes to 40-41
Port 14
Pottle F 136-137
'Private realm' 50, 56
Private renting: *see* Housing

Privatisation 54
   and education services 123-124, 125
   of housing 91
   of public space 54-55
Public realm 50-51, 56
   *see also* Urban public realm
Public service sector 16, 23, 30, 31
Public services 30, 31
Public space 7-9
**Public space and civility in London
   47-66**
Public transport: *see* British Rail,
   Bus(es), London Underground
Punter J 49


Q


Qualifications 16, 22
**The quality of London life 1-12**


R


Raban J 58-59, 62
Rail: *see* British Rail, London
   Underground
Religion,
   and education 120
Religious education 108
Rent(s), housing 89-90, 91, 92, 93, 95
Rented housing: *see* Housing
Repossession, housing 90, 92, 103
Retailing, change in 54
Richmond 5
Ridley, Tony 4, 76-77
Ridley T M and Travers T 79
Ridley T M and Tresidder J O 73-74
Road pricing 76, 78
Roads 75-76, 78
   *see also* Car(s)
Royal Institution of Chartered
   Surveyors 85, 103
Rykwert J 55-56


S


St. Pancras Station 140, 141, 146
School inspectors, inspection 111,
   123-124, 127
Segregation,
   residential 13
   spacial 19

Sennett R 49
SERPLAN 77
Services, service sector 14, 15, 22
Shankland G *et al* 31
Simmel G 49, 58, 59
Simpson A 62
Single European Market, SEM 19, 30
Skogan W G 41
Social housing: *see Housing*
Suburbs, suburbanisation 52-53, 54, 63
    *see also* decentralisation
Sunday Times, The 4
Svanholm B O 68-69


**T**

Taylor N 56, 63
Teachers, school 124-125
Tenure: *see* Housing
Thatcherism 3
Tibbalds F 61
Times, The 76
Tindall G 62, 147
Townsend P *et al* 31
Training 5, 27-28, 31
Trains: *see* British Rail
**Transport** 67-81
Transport 3-6, 30, 67-81, 102, 144
Transport employment 21-22, 23
Transport planning 72, 79-80
Transport policy 78-79
Travel patterns in London 69-71
Travers *et al* 10
Tomlinson, Sir Bernard 7
Tyler P 15


**U**

Underclass 2, 3, 29

Underground 4
    *also see* London Underground
Unemployment 4, 16-17, 19-20, 24, 27,
    30, 31
Urban planning: *see* Planning
Urban public realm 47-52


**V**

**A view of London life** 133-151
Vocational qualifications 121


**W**

Wages
Wandsworth 115-125, 126
Waters C 52
Webb B 138
Whitehead C M E 8, 83, 92
Whitehead C M E and Cross D T 98,
    104
Whitehead C M E and Kleinman M P
    91, 92
Wirth L 49, 58, 62
Wolff M 15, 59
'World city' 4, 15, 80


**Y**

Young, K 2, 8, 9, 62, 63, 140
Young K and Garside P 54, 63
Young K and Kramer J 53
Young K G and Mills L 18


**Z**

Zimbardo P 61